THE SIMPLE TOUCH OF FATE

THE SIMPLE TOUCH OF FATE

❖

How the Hand of Fate Touched Our Lives Forever

Real People; Real Stories
Edited by Arlene Uslander and
Brenda Warneka

iUniverse, Inc.
New York Lincoln Shanghai

THE SIMPLE TOUCH OF FATE
How the Hand of Fate Touched Our Lives Forever

iUniverse, Inc.

For information address:
iUniverse, Inc.
2021 Pine Lake Road, Suite 100
Lincoln, NE 68512
www.iuniverse.com

First printing

Cover design by Ronald L. Harmon.

MICHELANGELO. Detail from "Creation of Adam," portion of the Sistine Ceiling. 1508-12. Fresco.

ISBN: 0-595-30283-1

Printed in the United States of America

Contents

Acknowledgments

This book took more than four years to put together—from a small seed germinating in an editor's mind to more than 50 stories, selected with great care from hundreds of submissions. Perhaps the process of collecting stories for an anthology can be compared to giving birth—the pain and the joy.

We suffered through countless computer crashes, spent numerous hours researching supposedly "true" stories that turned out to be fiction, or that contained "factual" information that was incorrect, and spent many more hours editing and re-editing. We also went through the frustrating search for new e-mail addresses when we found that those we originally had on file for some of our writers were no longer valid.

But, there was also the joy and excitement of receiving wonderful stories from all over the world, getting to know many of the writers through the Internet, and actually becoming friends—even with people whose stories we unfortunately could not use in this book, but hopefully will in the next.

We want to express our deep appreciation and thanks to you, the story contributors, for your patience (your willingness to re-write and answer our seemingly endless questions, in our efforts to make sure we had the facts straight) and for your encouragement, support and loyalty. We hope that someday we can meet and thank each of you in person.

Our husbands, Ira and Dick, you have been unbelievably patient, and helpful in so many ways—assisting us with research, giving objective opinions and critiques (*when asked*); coming to our rescue when we had MAJOR computer problems, and putting up with the long hours we spent at the computer—hours we were unable to spend with you. Thank you for being there when we needed you, and for *not* being there (and not complaining) when we needed the time and space to work on this project on our own. And thank you for leaving a little bit of merchandise on the shelves, and not depleting our entire savings accounts when you went "discount" shopping together while we toiled away.

Special thanks, also to you, dear friends, Ronald Harmon, artist, author and photographer, who designed the book cover; and Rusty Fischer, writer, public relations man, and Internet maven. Ron, you have been helpful in so many ways, besides designing the cover—contributing quotes, and giving great support and encouragement for this project. Rusty, you were called upon for advice again and again, which you gave most willingly and graciously. Your experience as an established writer, editor, and frequent contributor to anthologies was invaluable to us.

We would also like to thank you, Beth Fowler, story contributor, for helping spread the word that we were looking for submissions. Your advice as a prolific, well-respected writer was also most helpful.

We thank you, Larry Hicks and Jacob Herbst, subjects of two of our stories, for giving of your time and allowing us to interview you. We felt that you each had a compelling story to tell, and with your patient help, we were able to tell it.

To all whom we have mentioned, and to many others—those of you who led us to people who had stories to share; consultants whose advice we sought and received on technical matters, and to friends and family who believed in us and our idea for the book—thank you for helping us "keep the faith" to keep on going with FATE.

Some of the names and places in the stories that follow have been changed to protect the privacy of those involved.

Preface

A businessman visiting the United States from Israel is scheduled to depart from Boston to Los Angeles the following morning at 8:45. Circumstances intervene and he misses his flight—American Airlines, Flight 11 to Los Angeles. The date is September 11, 2001.

A young man returns home from a date with his girlfriend, goes to bed and falls asleep. He is alone in the house. Shortly after midnight, he awakens with a blinding headache, and collapses onto the floor. He ends up being saved from death by a coincidence—or was it Fate?

A tired nurse, finishing up the night shift, decides to stay on duty a little longer to assist *one more* patient, brought in as an emergency, and is in for an incredible shock when she learns who the patient is.

A retired Marine decides to stay home for the evening, instead of going to a movie as he and his wife had discussed doing. When a private plane plunges into a lake near his home, the scene is set for him to use his highly specialized search and rescue skills learned in the military to become a hero, saving the life of a celebrity. Just a fortunate coincidence that the couple decided against a movie, and that the Marine happened to have been trained in underwater airplane search and rescue...or the hand of Fate extending its fingers to create a miracle?

It was hearing stories like these, as well as thinking about incidents that happened in our own lives, that started us to question: Are these happenings random chance, mere accidents, simple coincidence—or is there really such a thing as "Fate?"

Sometimes we experience odd circumstances that seem to be more than coincidence, and we can't help but ask ourselves, "Was that simply the luck of the draw, or was it *meant to be?*"

In *Conversations with God, Book I,* Neale Donald Walsch says, "Nothing happens by accident in God's world; there is no such thing as coincidence. Nor is the world buffeted by random choice. There is only a grand design."

While compiling the stories for this book, we learned that the word "Fate" means many different things to different people. To one person, it means having a last minute change of mind or heart before boarding a plane, a train, or a car that crashed. To another, it means simply taking a different turn in the road, or having a chance meeting with an individual that changed his or her whole life forever! To still others, the word "Fate" means that some other person happened to be at the right place, at the right time *for* them, and in that sense, turned out to be a mentor, an earthly angel—a guiding light.

This book is about all these different kinds of Fate. The stories are represented as true by the authors and their sources. Although the circumstances are all different, and the authors are from all walks of life, and from different parts of the world, the common thread is that each story raises the question: "Was that just a coincidence—or was it meant to be?"

Most of the contributors to this anthology have been previously published. Several have had stories represented in well-known anthologies, such as the *Chicken Soup* series; *A Cup of Comfort; Chocolate for Women,* and *Angel Animals.* Among the authors are college professors, a physician, an attorney, a psychologist, newspaper editor, stock analyst, photographer, publications and communications specialist, teachers, musicians, artists, businessmen and-women, grandparents, housewives, househusbands, and many others. The one thing they all have in common is their fascination with "Fate."

About the Editors

When I (Arlene) first got the idea of putting together a collection of stories about "fate," I posted an announcement on a writers' web site, soliciting submissions. I received only one response, from a person named Brenda. She wanted to know whether an experience involving her husband would be appropriate for my book. She described the incident, and I e-mailed her back, saying that it sounded just like what I was looking for. About a week later, she sent me the story. It was perfect for the anthology.

Having received the one story, I was confident that I would get more, and I realized that I needed a good query letter to present my idea to agents or publishers. However, even though I am the author of a number of published books, writing query letters has never been one of my strong suits, so I decided to post another announcement on the same writers' web site, asking if anyone could help me write a query letter. Again, I received only one response, which said, "How could you have had books published if you can't write a good query letter?" And, once again, it was signed "Brenda."

I thought that was kind of a cheeky response, and felt I had to defend myself, so I e-mailed Brenda back, explaining that just because one can write a good book, doesn't *necessarily* mean that one can write a good query letter. She e-mailed me back; I, in turn, e-mailed her back, and that was the beginning of our e-mail friendship.

Because that was more than four years ago, some of the details of our early e-mails are not clear in my mind. We both remember, though, that I asked Brenda to give me her personal e-mail address, and she asked me for mine, as so far, we had been contacting each other through a writers' web site.

We started writing each other once a week or so, telling each other about our families, our work, our vacations—the kinds of things most women talk about when they first become acquainted. The fact that we live in different parts of the country, she in Arizona, I in Illinois, and that our work experience has been totally different—she is an attorney; I was an elementary school teacher for most of my adult life, and am a free-lance editor—didn't seem to get in the way of our e-mail friendship at all. If anything, it enhanced it. I was learning about the "trials" and tribulations of a lawyer's life, never having had an attorney for a friend, and I think she was interested in my writing career, since she, too, is a writer.

After e-mailing back and forth for about a year and a half, we decided it was time to meet. It just so happened that my husband and I, and Brenda and her husband, were going to be in Florida at approximately the same time, so we decided the four of us should meet for a weekend.

My husband and I picked up Brenda and her husband at the hotel where they were staying, which was only a few blocks from the house I had rented for my family. Having exchanged pictures, we easily recognized the other. We greeted each other warmly, introduced our husbands, and from that moment on, it was as though we had been friends all our lives. What made everything even nicer was that our husbands discovered they had so much in common. They both are businessmen; they like to fish; they love to cook, and have a great time browsing through kitchen equipment stores, specialty food shops, hardware and electronic stores, and factory outlets.

When I returned from Florida, my colleagues at work were eager to find out how I liked my "e-mail buddy," as they called her. Most of them were surprised that I would actually make vacation plans with someone I had met on the Internet. "How do you know you can trust someone you meet online?" several people asked me. "How do you know that what they tell you about themselves is the truth?" asked others. One even went so far as to say, "She could be an ax murderess!"

I simply pointed out that at my stage of life, I consider myself a fairly good judge of character. I mean, after all, it wasn't like I was some daring teenager, looking for thrills. After my trip to Florida, I confirmed to my colleagues that Brenda was just as nice as I had thought she was before we met. "In fact," I added, "she is everything I could ever want in a friend."

About a year after I met Brenda in person, I asked her if she would consider being the co-editor of this book. I thought it would be fun to work on it (albeit long distance) together. Her response was short and (not so) sweet: "NO, NO, NO!" She explained that she was much too busy with work, family, friends and various activities, to take on still another project. Somehow, though, after a lot of cajoling, pleading and *begging,* I was able to convince her. What I didn't realize until after Brenda started working with me, is what an outstanding editor she is. So, I got much more than I bargained for: a fun co-editor, superb editing skills, and someone to help with the story selection.

The fact that Brenda was the first one (actually the only one) to send in a story in response to my announcement on that particular writers' web site, and ended up being my co-editor, and very good friend, seems to me like kind of a fate story in itself—like she just happened to be trolling along the Internet late one night, at the right place, at the right time, and got hooked by my "intriguing" fate announcement.

So, what you are about to read are stories we both selected from hundreds that were submitted, and if you notice any typos, or misspellings, they are my fault (Arlene's) not Brenda's!

We would like to invite you to share your own fate stories with us for possible use in our next book. For information, e-mail Arlene at auslander@theramp.net, visit her web site: www.theramp.net/auslander, or write to her at 1920 Chestnut Avenue, #105, Glenview, Illinois, 60025. You can e-mail Brenda at warneka@cox.net or write to her at 6128 E. Cactus Wren Road, Paradise Valley, Arizona 85253.

We also would be interested in hearing which are your favorite stories in this book. Please feel free to e-mail or write to us.

What is Fate?

Luck of the draw, or meant to be? Our lives are impacted by forces we cannot explain, often changed for reasons we will never totally understand. However, when people are touched by the hand of fate, they know it. Whether fate brings them their heart's desire, or forever closes the door to their dreams, the path that has brought them to that point is clear, and fate's irony is unmistakable.

Thomas Wilson (writer, musician, philosopher)

Jacob! Jacob!
Reborn September 11, 2001

Jacob Herbst was not unfamiliar with the sight of death and destruction. Living in Israel from the time he was three years old, he had seen much fighting and killing. As a young man, Jacob had fought in wars. But he had never been so close to dying as he was on September 11th, 2001. What he saw on television that day was something he never imagined he would see in his lifetime. The fact that his own life almost ended on September 11th, here in the United States, but did not, because of some strange "touch of fate" is a thought he will carry with him for the rest of his days; "a thought that still brings moisture" to his eyes.

A computer engineer by trade, Jacob is founder and CEO of FilesX, a software development company located in Boston. Although he lives in Israel, Jacob travels to the United States frequently on business. He arrived in Boston on September 9th. On the evening of September 10th, he met with his good friend and business consultant, Steve Duplessie, founder and Senior Analyst of ESG (Enterprise Storage Group), a consulting and marketing firm located in Milford, 30 miles west of Boston. The purpose of the visit was to do some brainstorming about the direction of FilesX, and the hiring of a vice president of sales.

"We didn't come up with the names of any candidates who sounded like they would fill the bill," said Jacob, "so I thanked Steve very much, said we would talk further, and I bid him good night."

ESG is housed on the top floor of a small two-story building, and as Jacob walked through the parking lot, he heard his name being called, "Jacob! Jacob!"

Jacob turned and saw Steve waving at him to come back upstairs, which he did. Steve told Jacob that he had thought of someone who might be just the person for vice president of sales. His name was Michael Beaudet. Steve called Michael while Jacob was there, suggested that Michael might want to interview with Jacob, and said that Jacob would be in touch with him.

Jacob's time was already scheduled for the rest of the evening, and he was leaving Boston the next morning for Los Angeles, where he would visit with friends before going on to the Silicon Valley for business. After he left Steve, he thought to himself, *Ah, should I call Michael tonight or should I not?*

"But" recalled Jacob, "something told me I should call, so I left a message on Michael's voice mail, asking if we could meet later that evening. Michael called me back while I was at a dinner meeting, and said, 'I can't meet you tonight, but I can meet you very early tomorrow morning,' so we scheduled our meeting for 6:00 a.m."

The flight Jacob was scheduled to take the following morning was due to depart from Boston's Logan Airport at 8:45—American Airlines, Flight 11, to Los Angeles.

"The meeting with Michael was excellent," said Jacob, "but it took longer than I had anticipated. I barely had time to catch the flight; it is about an hour's drive from our office to the airport, but still I decided I would try to make it."

However, traffic slowed him down more than he had expected, and as Jacob was getting closer to the airport in his rental car, he realized that he had already missed his flight. He thought he would go on to the airport to try to get on the next flight. It was now about ten minutes past nine. Then, all of a sudden, he heard on the car radio that a plane had hit the World Trade Center in New York City.

"First I thought it was a sick joke," said Jacob. "You know how some people say bizarre things when they call in on radio talk shows. And then I thought that maybe it was a small private plane like the one that hit the Empire State Building a few years ago. However, they then announced that it was a passenger plane, and a few minutes later, reported that the second plane had hit; it was American Airlines, Flight 11, bound for Los Angeles. *The plane I was supposed to be on.* As you can imagine, I was in great shock!"

Jacob wondered what he should do. Should he go to the airport and try to take a later flight…or what? He decided to go back to the hotel and try to find out what was happening. The first thing he did when he got there, however, was call Michael Beaudet.

"I called to thank you, Mike," said Jacob. Mike thought Jacob was calling to thank him for the meeting. He said, "Jacob, do you have any idea what is going on? Look at the TV!" Jacob said, "Yes, I know what is going on, and I would like to thank you for saving my life. If you had been able to meet with me last night, I would have been on the American Airlines flight that crashed into the Twin Towers."

Jacob continued to watch what was happening on TV. "It was terrible—a horrible sight!" he recalls. All the airports were shut down, so Jacob did not get back to Israel until September 15th. He was able to contact his family—not by telephone because there was no phone access, but by e-mail, "which shows you," pointed out Jacob, "how important the Internet is."

However, more important to Jacob, husband of Michaela, father of four grown children and two young grandchildren, is the lesson he learned from his close brush with death. He thinks about September 11th a lot, "and," he says, "it is still not so easy. I have learned to postpone personal plans less, especially ones I really want to make. Let's say you want to go some place nice with your family, or spend more time with your kids, and you tend to put it off. You say, 'Oh, we can do that another time. I have business to take care of.' I realize now it is possible there might not *be* another time. Let's do it *now*. Go on a nice trip. Go with the grandkids. Tomorrow is nothing that is very secure anymore, so I am less apt to put things off. You can plan very well, but it isn't always within your control.

"The experience also helped me to put more balance into my life—to be more aware of priorities. I still put a high priority on business when needed, but I make more time for other things as well."

When he is in the United Sates at the FilesX office, Jacob sees Michael Beaudet every day, and he often thanks Michael for saving his life.

When Michael tells the story, according to Jacob, he says, "I knew when Jacob called to thank me for saving his life that fateful morning, I had gotten the job!"

"This is the first time that I have talked extensively about that day," Jacob said when interviewed for this story. "I consider that I was reborn on September, 11th, 2001."

Yes, it is true that Michael Beaudet had much to do with Jacob's "rebirth," because he could not meet with Jacob the night before, and the meeting went on longer than anticipated the next morning. And the traffic slowed Jacob down on his way to the airport. Yet, equally responsible is Steve Duplessie, who called out through the open window, "Jacob, Jacob!" What if Steve had not suddenly thought of Michael Beaudet for the job?

Or, what if Jacob had not heard him call and had gone on into the night...?

By Arlene Uslander

Arlene Uslander is the author of 14 non-fiction books, and has had more than 400 articles published in newspapers and magazines. She has won several media awards for "Excellence in Journalism." She and her husband, Ira, reside in Glenview, Illinois. They have two sons and three grandchildren. Besides her great love of writing, she enjoys editing, music, traveling, golf and theater. Arlene says she has aged ten years while putting this anthology together, so some of her longtime friends no longer recognize her.

Journey to Healing

Fate is the symphony of our choices—but WHO is the director?

Sleepy Time tea is boiling on the stove, and I am about to go to bed, winding down after a long day as the Emergency Medical Services Director for the Pacific Island of Guam.

"How did you choose to go into medicine?" you ask.

My thoughts drift back to my conservative high school in Germany. This is the place where I developed my first intense, longing career dreams, but medicine was not one of them. My dreams centered on becoming a circus acrobat. I fantasized about lifting people out of their daily lives with beautiful, artistic stunts. I wanted the audience's imagination to soar with me under the ceiling of the circus tent, temporarily leaving all worries and pains behind.

To my parents' credit, they never made fun of my circus dreams. They did suggest that I visit a career-counseling center to explore alternatives. I followed their advice, and the career counselor suggested that I become, not a circus acrobat, but a physician.

The career counselor's suggestion left me in a state of turmoil. I felt disappointed that she had not supported my circus acrobat dream; yet, I also felt a shy pride and a strange excitement about the thought of becoming a doctor.

As I walked home, however, mounting fears replaced that fleeting pride and excitement about a career in medicine. A doctor? Not a circus acrobat? By the time I arrived home, I had dismissed the career counselor's suggestion. The circus tent seemed to be a much more beautiful place to work than the white, sterile corridors of a hospital.

Also, the memory of my incredibly old, female childhood pediatrician made me feel that a career in medicine would mean giving up my youth, beauty, and feminine qualities. Finally, I simply was critical of the field itself; hesitant because I had heard people complain that modern medicine was no longer a healing profession because it viewed disease in terms of body parts, and not patients.

A few months later, my circus dreams were shattered. I found out that I was too old to be accepted into the acrobat school in Scotland upon which I had been counting. It was the only acrobat school that I was aware of, so a lonely post-high school period ensued during which I wondered what I should do with my life.

I agonized over the career counselor's suggestion. Did she know something that I did not know? I finally entered college where, much to my own surprise, I felt compelled to include pre-medical courses in my potpourri of studies that ranged from yoga and gymnastics to film writing and philosophy.

The time came to either apply or not apply to medical school. I decided that it never had been my own idea to study medicine. What would I have become if I had never gone to the career counselor? Certainly not a physician.

I decided against medicine and, instead, pursued a Master's Degree in Cybernetics (the study of the management of complex systems).

I enjoyed the cybernetics program very much and would have become a consultant in that field had it not been for another turn of events. One day, during a visit to my doctor, he asked me, "Have you ever thought about studying medicine? You would be a fine doctor." For some reason, it felt as though his question was opening an old wound.

I shared my concerns about medicine with the doctor, and told him that my current career choice was final. I did not tell him about the years I had spent during my undergraduate studies debating and re-debating whether or not I should become a doctor. I also did not let him know that even now, after having chosen another career, something continued to tug at the very core of my being every time I crossed paths with medicine.

During my next appointment, the doctor introduced me to an unusually attractive young lady. She was a physician! She was a fascinating lady, very intelligent, and also beautiful and caring. She glowed when describing her job. She was quite different from my old childhood pediatrician who had been my only previous female physician role model. I truly enjoyed my conversation with this young doctor, and I went home with nagging feelings that my preconceived notions about medicine might be false.

When I returned for a follow-up visit, my doctor had an application for medical school in his office. He handed it to me, and said, "You do whatever you think is right for you, but this year's deadline for applying to medical school is rapidly approaching. I brought these forms in case you want to give it a try."

After much contemplation, I filled out the forms. Due to financial restrictions, I was only able to complete the application process to one school, the UCLA Medical School. To my surprise, I was accepted. I once again wavered about my ability to be a physician. But, before I could again turn my back on medical school, another turn of events occurred.

I had partly financed my graduate studies by being a live-in manager of an apartment house in a low-income area. For years, I had successfully juggled the demands of the landlord for punctual rent collection against the complete disinterest of the tenants in paying on a timely basis. But just a few weeks before the beginning of medical school, and with only my Master's thesis left to write, I, for the first time, encountered threats of violence from two tenants while trying to collect rent from them. Faced with an increasingly unsafe living arrangement, and encouraged by UCLA to join their medical school, I decided to move to Los Angeles and write my thesis there, while giving medical school a try.

When I entered medical school, I found my childhood fears about medicine surfacing one more time. This time, however, fate brought a conclusion to the issue. Norman Cousins, a famous journalist and writer who had written a book about the value of humor in the healing process, gave a lecture that I attended during my first few months of medical school. He talked about medicine from a patient's perspective, and about how physicians often tend to the patient's body, but forget the patient's soul. He said one cannot heal without the other. I was on the edge of my chair. Here was a man who was addressing the heart of my concerns about medicine. I asked many questions during the lecture.

Sensing my interest, Norman Cousins sought me out after class and invited me to lunch. I was deeply honored and spilled out my fears to him that modern medicine really might no longer be a healing profession. I confessed my serious doubts about continuing medical school. Finally, he said, "There is a need in the medical field for people with your kind of doubts and questions. What would it take for you to commit?"

I thought for a long time (he finished his lunch) and finally answered, "I used to have this philosophy professor at San Jose University who really inspired me. If *he* were to tell me that medical school was the right thing for me, then I would finish."

"So," Norman Cousins asked, "how do you get in touch with your professor?"

Sadly, I told him, this professor had left for Sweden several years before, and I no longer knew his whereabouts. Norman Cousins said that if I could locate this professor, he would pay for me to telephone him, or even visit him, in Sweden.

I left the restaurant in deep thought and started to drive home, trying to remember to which city in Sweden my philosophy professor had moved. Suddenly, I slammed on the brakes. I had carelessly entered a pedestrian crosswalk while deep in thought. A man was in the crosswalk and had been nudged slightly by my car. With my whole body shaking uncontrollably, I got out to see if he was hurt.

The pedestrian I had nearly knocked over was my philosophy professor from San Jose State University! He was on a layover between airline flights, on his way back to Sweden, and had decided to come into the UCLA area to buy some shoelaces.

With tears streaming down my face, I asked him whether or not I should become a doctor. He instantly recognized me. He did not even mention that I could have killed him, and that my car was now blocking traffic, with other drivers honking incessantly. When he said in a stern voice, "Yes, Andrea, you should become a doctor," I finally found the courage to commit.

Today, I love being a physician. I specialize in emergency medicine and prehospital emergency care, which my friends view as one of the more "ugly" and less feminine branches of medicine. But, I no longer have my childhood fears. To me, this is a most beautiful profession.

Healing does take place in modern medicine. Healing takes place everywhere. It happens any time that people care about one another. And, aesthetics abound in medicine. It only takes seeing people for their souls, rather than their body parts.

As I drink my Sleepy Time tea and reflect on the day, I again thank those who stood in my way when I was trying to turn my back on this most honorable profession.

By Andrea Eberly

Andrea Eberly, MD, is an emergency medicine physician who served as the Medical Director of the Pacific Island of Guam's Emergency Medical Services for several years. She recently moved back to the States where she is taking a break to be a wife and mother. Guam is never far from her thoughts, though, and she hopes to return with her family one day.

Miracle in Alexandria

Yet who shall shut out fate?

—Edwin Arnold

Life is a series of big and small miracles! We tend to take them for granted, but there are some that stay in our minds forever.

My family, Russian in origin, immigrated to Alexandria, Egypt, from their homeland in 1920. I was born the following year. We were stateless since we were never required to become Egyptian citizens, and were under the protection of the Royal House of Egypt. However, when Farouk, the last King of Egypt, was overthrown and exiled in 1956, we were uneasy as to our future, even though we did not belong to the group of Faro supporters who were being deported.

It was April 1958: Alexandria was in turmoil. Following the war with Israel, there was a general exodus of foreign nationals, such as English, French and anybody of the Jewish faith. The political climate in the country was strongly fomented by Moslem extremists who were putting pressure on the authorities to get rid of all foreigners on Egyptian soil.

My father was a captain with the Anglo-Egyptian police, and continued as such after the takeover of the country by the military headed by General Mohammed Neguib and later by Colonel Abdel Nasser. However, we decided to seek refuge in the United States. The Russian quota, being very small, allowed us to obtain American visas in record time. Father put in his resignation, but stress and worry took their toll, and he had a near-fatal heart attack. He recuperated slowly, but kept his spirits high, knowing he was about to take his family out of a country where we were no longer welcome.

One morning close to our departure date, my father and I took a taxi to the passport office to collect our papers. We would then proceed downtown to the shipping company that was sending our heavy trunks full of books and personal articles to the United States. We were also to collect our passage tickets on the boat that was taking us to New York because Father's health did not permit him to fly. We had a large amount of money with us, since we could not write checks, as our British bank account was sequestrated (though we were able to withdraw our savings just in time), and all transactions had to be made in cash. I carried a large leather attaché case containing our precious American visas, the money, and my father's big police revolver, still in its halter, which was to be returned to his office the same day.

We asked the taxi driver to wait for us while we collected the passports, which we then placed in the attaché case, and directed the driver to go to the shipping company on Sherif Pasha Street, in the center of the busy downtown area. Father was very nervous because we were carrying the revolver. During those dangerous days, it was a criminal offense to carry any firearm, and people were pitilessly jailed for less than that. However, we hoped that we would soon consign the revolver to the Central Precinct before anyone would spot it.

We arrived at our destination and went up the ancient elevator to the third floor of the massive old building, built at the turn of the century. Greeted by the friendly manager of the shipping company, Father sank into a comfortable chair and turned to me to hand him the attaché case. For a long moment, I stared at my father's face while my mind tried to cope with the realization that we no longer had the attaché case!

We looked at each other in horror, unable to speak. I had believed that Father was holding the case, while he thought I was carrying it. While getting out of the taxi and paying the driver, neither of us noticed that the attaché case was left in the taxi!

Father leaned back in his chair and closed his eyes. I knew the loss of the attaché case meant that we had lost everything. We already had sold our house, our furniture and our car. Our passports, our only identification now, were gone. Our money, our American visas, and, more ominously, the service revolver were gone.

There was little hope of the taxi driver ever returning the contents of the attaché case. Even the most honest of men would be too frightened to admit that he had a revolver which could land him directly in jail.

Unwilling to wait for the elevator, I rushed down the stairs and into the busy street. All taxis were yellow, and there were dozens of them speeding in opposite directions while I looked around in despair. The sidewalks were crowded with shoppers and peddlers who jostled me. I prayed to God, unable to remember any proper words of prayer, but hoping He would understand my turmoil and helplessness.

I jumped as a hand grabbed my arm, and I looked into the laughing face of a friend of ours, whose office was in the business district. "Hey," he said, "what the heck are you doing here instead of packing your belongings?" I could not control the tears that streamed down my face as I told him in a few jumbled sentences what had happened. He questioned me as to whether I remembered anything about the taxi or the driver, but all I could tell him was that we had picked him up on the street and asked him to wait for us at the passport office.

My friend hailed a passing taxi and told the driver to go to the passport office; this was our only clue, weak as it was. Arriving at the intersection of the government office, we saw a long line of yellow taxis, all identical, all drivers looking like clones of our fateful driver! We got out of our taxi and started walking toward the waiting taxis.

All of a sudden, one of the taxi drivers thrust his head through his window and shouted, "Mademoiselle, Mademoiselle, where do you want to go this time? I'll take you!" I thought I would pass out from the anxiety. We rushed toward the taxi, and my friend quickly opened the back door. There, flat on the floor, half-concealed under the back of the driver's seat, lay our precious attaché case, still bulging with its priceless contents.

I will never forget the expression of disappointment on the face of the taxi driver when he saw us pull out the attaché case and realized that he had failed to spot it. However, since he did not know what he had missed, we did not tell him. He accepted a generous tip and happily drove away, while I suddenly realized that God had indeed heard me, although I had forgotten the proper words of prayer for this occasion.

I went back to the shipping company where I knew a moment of pure joy when I handed over the attaché case to my dear father, who just held me in his arms for a while, wiping away my tears with his gentle hand.

By Vicka Markov Surovtsov

Vicka Surovtsov, nee Markov, was born in Egypt. She has an MA in French and Russian, has traveled extensively in Europe and Latin America and speaks five languages. She is married to George Surovtsov and they live in Northern California. Vicka's hobbies are portrait painting and writing. Her first book, a memoir, *Amigos & Friends,* is about their life in Mexico. She is working at present on her second book, depicting life in a small Russian community in Egypt after World War I.

Better Lucky Than Good

Fate is the ultimate trickster. It often has the King when the Queen is played and then for a lark, it plays the three when you have the four. Often skill is not the determinant of the outcome; it is just dumb luck. Yes, and the brilliance is often coincidence—or is it?

As I boarded the Long Island Railroad commuter train on my way to work at the New York Stock Exchange, I was thinking that stock trading, in spite of recent technological changes, is still nothing but a game of chance. There are millions to be made, and millions to be lost. My father was a trader who owned a seat on the exchange. He wasn't the best at his job or the worst, but he did manage to raise a family comfortably.

Taking my seat on the train next to the window, I reflected on how the stock market's recent volatility was causing so much pain to the average investor. When it's on its way up, people love it too much, and when it's going down, they shut their eyes. The crazed emotions that greed creates make the business. The new computer-driven agents amplify the gyrations. At times, I would be on top of the situation and on the right side, and then, as fast as a microprocessor could spit-out orders, I was "under the ice." This new way of doing things was disconcerting. I often wondered what my old man would make of it.

As the train rolled onward, the New York City skyline came into view. My stomach tightened; I was nearing the battleground. My pulse raced as the spires of commerce neared. I would soon have to decide how to play the market. Should I be a buyer or a seller? I always thumbed through my print-out of current positions at this point. Today, it seemed that I might be a bit on the long side. This could be dangerous. I glanced at the newspaper of the fellow setting next to me. The headline screamed "New Financial Millennia Coming." There were also articles about a White House sex scandal and North Korea testing missiles.

"Well," I mused, "if it's in the *New York Times*, everyone knows it already." Luckily, my wife was now working, and, if I screwed up, we could still last awhile. I was wondering how much longer I could continue in this business. The stress was killing me. The hours were short—we started at 9:30 a.m. and got out at 4:00 p.m.—but the time in-between seemed eternal. I needed a way out. I had to make the big hit: the last big score that would allow me to clip coupons from treasury bonds the rest of my life.

I ran the plan through my mind. It would be the final battle—I would margin to the hilt and shoot it all. An all-or-nothing stratagem began to formulate in my mind as the train pulled into Penn Station. My thoughts were distracted by the masses of commuters rushing from the train to catch the subway. It was chaos. Briefcases and umbrellas were flying.

This was not a time to formulate a detailed strategy. I picked up my laptop and scurried off the train. I was in a hurry along with everyone else. Suddenly, I felt a push from behind. I looked down and saw a coin, then stooped to pick it up. It was a silver dollar. I laughed and put it in my pocket. Then, as I came up to the newsstand, I turned to the vendor.

"One Quick Pick lottery ticket, please. I just found this dollar; this could be my lucky day." I was laughing as I finished the sentence. The vendor gave me the ticket without so much as a nod. I folded it, put it in my pocket, and hurried onto the subway train.

I was sweating; my heart was beating faster and faster. Wall Street grew closer and closer. It was not a heart attack, but the rising tension was not subsiding either. I clutched my laptop for dear life. Wall Street was the next stop.

I exited the subway. As I walked, I looked into other traders' faces for signs. The signs were mixed. I was almost frozen in fear. As I neared the exchange, I wanted out. The neon sign of a nearby bar caught my eye. It was calling me big-time, but I would not allow myself to go in this early in the day. I lit a smoke to relax. I leaned against an old building to steady myself.

Suddenly, as if by magic, I came up with a plan. I was going to go long on IBM shares. Yes, that was it. Shoot the moon; the trade was now coming. I would buy it on the opening bell, and if those computers went my way, I would be out of there at four o'clock and in the chips. Filled with self-confidence, I finished my cigarette and entered the exchange building.

Big John from Merrill Lynch filled the order and looked at me as though he thought I was crazy. Maybe I was, but I felt I would be the one laughing on settlement day. Then an announcement crossed the tape, **"Greenspan resigns."** The buzz was incredible and the market tanked. Not dropped, but *tanked*. The flood of sell orders from the computers was relentless. The stocks were dropping like rockets.

"Oh, hell!" I muttered. I was caught on the wrong side of the trade. Then I decided to execute the second leg of the trade. "Selling 10,000 IBM's at market!" I screamed desperately into the crowd.

"Be careful, guy. This is a fast market." Big John shook his head as he filled the order. Now I was cash-strapped. I had to liquidate more long positions. Rapidly, I began to go from post to post, selling myself out to cover my margin commitment. The market was falling faster and faster. My head was spinning. Then another buzz passed on the broad tape: **"Correction—Greenspan not resigning."** The computers reversed positions and drove the market higher.

I was wiped out. My instincts had betrayed me. Realizing the damage was done, I called it a day and walked across the street into the bar.

"Double vodka and beer chaser," I bellowed.

"Hey, it's only 10 a.m. You sure?" asked the bartender. He had seen this look before. He got the drinks.

"Bad day, huh?" he said slowly as he set the glasses on the counter. "Well, stuff happens; maybe tomorrow will be better."

"Yeah," I said, and carried my drink over to a table. I wasn't in the mood to talk to anyone.

After a few rounds, things got hazy. I left the bar and went to the subway. I don't remember much of the trip home. When I got there, I went to bed. I had missed supper with the family. On bad trading days, they knew better than to bother me. I woke up in the middle of the night and made my way to the computer to see the damages.

My brokerage accounts came up on the computer screen; the balances were severely drawn down. Major trouble! I sat on the couch and began to cry. I went for my suit jacket, rummaging through the pockets for cigarettes. Suddenly, I found the Lotto ticket. I laughed hysterically, went back to the computer again, logged onto the Lotto web site, and began to check the numbers.

Pencil in hand, I started circling the numbers. Four, yes, I have that; 6, yes, I have that; 18, yes, I have that. I began to perspire. Then 26, yes, I have that. I had won at least the four-number pool. But fate was not stopping there. I needed a 32 and, yes, I had it. I was in the five-number pool. Then, I screamed with joy—53. I hit the big one! Yes, the silver dollar I had found had bought the winning Lotto ticket.

My screams woke the whole house. My two daughters and wife rushed into the living room. I began to relate the tale, telling them how I had gotten whipsawed and had blown everything. Well, almost everything. Then I showed them the lottery ticket that had just made us rich. We all hugged and smiled at the Grace of the Fates.

By Dave Gitomer

Dave Gitomer is a New York poet who writes and has done performance poetry on the Internet, radio, and at cafes. He showcases his work on America Online and has been featured on *Poetic Spotlight*. He likes to read books on philosophy, especially those with an Eastern slant. Although written in first person, Dave points out that the story, "Better Lucky than Good" happened to a good friend of his. Does Dave buy lottery tickets? You will have to ask him.

Desert Boomerang

As we move through life, the force of fate creates events that we only appreciate when we reflect on our existence.

—Ronald Harmon

In 1991, as a shield was replaced by an angry storm, Saddam Hussein threatened America with the mother of all battles. In turn, President George Bush drew a line in the sand. That line was quickly wrapped around Iraq and used to choke the life out of thousands. As a U.S. Army MP, I was there when the Americans crossed the breach from Saudi Arabia into Iraq, crushing the first of three Iraqi lines of defense along the way. It was like someone had lifted the curtain to hell, giving everyone a free peek.

It took four days, or a mere 100 hours, before the ground war ended. History was made. In triumph, Kuwait was liberated, while Hussein was humiliated before the whole world. An unconditional withdrawal was ordered. Politically, the sadistic demon was slain. In reality, unlike thousands of his own people, he still lived. And, the war was far from over.

Two weeks after the last shots were fired, I was standing guard at a barren traffic control point in Iraq when a lone vehicle approached. It was American, so I waved it through. The driver pulled up to me and stopped. He was a black sergeant, and from the look in his eyes, he was definitely lost.

"Man, am I glad to see you!" he said with a nervous grin. "I lost my convoy in the dust storm that just passed through. I'm supposed to be on Main Supply Route Green, but…"

I chuckled. The entire area was my patrol and I could have driven the roads in Iraq blindfolded. "You're not that far off," I confirmed. "Right now, you're on MSR Blue, but this route runs parallel to MSR Green. Keep south for the next four miles or so, and when you reach a fork in the road, you've met up with Green."

The sergeant's face showed relief, and I was happy to help him. With a wave, he was on his way. I, on the other hand, returned to the boredom of the desert's miles and miles of solitary confinement.

Several very unpleasant months passed. One afternoon, in base camp, my platoon sergeant, Tony Rosini, approached. "Hey, kid, got any plans today?"

"Yeah, I think I'll head to the mall," I joked.

He chuckled. "In that case, you can give me a ride into Saudi Arabia. My knee's been acting up, so maybe they'll give me some pain killers. Either way, I could use the time away, and from the look of it, so could you."

"Whose vehicle?" I asked.

Tony never answered. He just slid into the passenger seat of his own "A Horse With No Name."

We were making good time, traveling down the dusty road at a fast clip. We joked and laughed; there were only 40 miles between the Saudi Arabian border and us. Before long, radio traffic ceased. We were out of range. I noticed we had been the only vehicle on the road since we left. I continually scanned the vast terrain to make sure we were alone. There were still members of Iraq's Republican Guard on the loose, soldiers who came out of hiding during the dark hours. The farther we drove, though, the less it mattered. We were only an hour from our destination and safety.

Several miles later, I slowed down. We'd hit a dust storm, a bad one. I could hardly see three feet past the windshield. In the blink of an eye, the blue sky turned a blinding orange, as the harsh winds of the open desert rearranged the landscape.

Maneuvering the Hum-V right and left, I slowed down even more on the snake-shaped trail. Squinting my eyes, I concentrated and drove on. Then the nightmare began.

Approximately 30 miles from the border, I heard the bang. I did not know the cause, but it was a loud crash that came from the right side of the vehicle. The cause didn't matter because the rest was out of my hands.

In super slow motion, the vehicle tipped left, toward the driver's side. The windshield cracked at the top, then spidered throughout the center. The desert spun in circles before my eyes. I felt something heavy smash into the back of my bare skull. It was an army field phone, flying around aimlessly until it found a target. The piercing pain quickly led to numbness. My tense body went limp.

I felt as if I was submerged in a pool of warm water. Unlike any peace I had ever experienced before, the sensation was heavenly. With no choice but to accept the comfort, my eyes slammed shut. In the briefest moment in time, I watched as my life played out before me. It was a slide show, with one vivid picture after another being brought into the light.

I was euphoric. I was at peace. Then, as if reality were given its last chance, I thought, *all of this, only to die in a Hum-V accident?* I fought it off with everything inside me. I didn't want death. It wasn't my time. I fought, but the struggle was brief. There was no more pain, no more peace and no more pictures. There was only darkness.

I opened my eyes and felt a methodical pain surge throughout my being. My entire body throbbed, but it was my left arm and neck that caused me to groan. Attempting to lift my heavy head, my mind twirled in circles, fogged from the pain and disoriented from the shock. Turning my head slowly, I looked down at my fingers, and my wedding band was missing. Turning right, I saw the Hum-V. It was almost 40 feet away, lying on its roof. It looked like a hapless turtle upside down, resting on its shell. With all my might, I pushed myself to my knees.

The Hum-V's motor screamed for help. It was running at full idle. Trying to clear my blurred vision, I choked on the smell of gas and oil that leaked from the wreck. I took two small, painful steps toward the Hum-V when I saw Tony.

Like a bat, my platoon sergeant hung upside down within the wreckage. He was suspended in mid-air by a seat belt and appeared unconscious. Tony was in trouble. He needed help. Picking up the pace, I ignored my own pain. "Get out! Tony, get out!" I shouted.

Tony never moved, but the motor seemed to hear me. It raced faster. Without hesitation, I dove into the Hum-V.

I was right. Tony was out cold. Instinctively, I unbuckled the safety belt and awkwardly pulled my friend out. He was dead weight, but I continued to drag him, hoping that I wasn't causing more damage. I couldn't tell if Tony's back or neck was broken. Then, I realized that I wasn't even sure whether he was alive. I dragged him faster.

A safe distance from the Hum-V, I laid Tony onto the warm sand and took his pulse. He was still alive. Feeling the greatest sense of relief, I was promptly reacquainted with my own pain. The intensity made me nauseous. I felt as if I was going to pass out, but fought it off. Though I wanted nothing more, there was no time for a nap. Tony was coming out of it. The motor in the jeep let out one last whine and seized to an eerie halt.

For a while, I just sat in the sand, with Tony's head in my lap. Tony talked in riddles. His gibberish told me that he was in shock. I treated the symptoms according to my army training: I loosened Tony's restrictive clothing and elevated his feet. I moistened his lips with water. Bending over, I shaded my platoon sergeant's face from the burning sun.

Unsure whether he could understand or not, I also began reassuring my friend. It was the biggest act of my life, but I promised, "Don't you worry, Tony. I'll get us out of this one. We'll be okay." The empty words drifted off into the lonely desert. I was overcome with guilt; after all, I was behind the wheel when the accident occurred.

"My God, Tony, what have I done?" I whispered. Tony never answered. He just mumbled and shivered from the cold. The shiver scared me. It was more than 90 degrees, and my friend was freezing. Removing my shirt, I covered my platoon sergeant's upper body, then headed back to the smashed Hum-V.

I needed to figure out a plan. The closer I got to the Hum-V, the easier it was to see that I was not responsible for what had happened. In the midst of the heavy dust storm, we had hit a boulder with the right front tire. The Hum-V flipped three or four times, completely crushing the driver's side. It finally landed on its roof. The driver's side door was lying 20 feet from the scene. My spine tingled when I saw it.

It was too bizarre to be coincidental. I wasn't wearing a helmet, which allowed the telephone to knock me out. In turn, my body was thrown around at will. My seat belt would have trapped me under the weight of the wreckage, but I had neglected to put it on. The door had flown off, throwing me out of the truck and away from the final landing. That was the clincher. If each element hadn't happened in sequence, I would have been smashed like a grape. For reasons unknown to me, I was still alive. It was no less than a miracle. From then on, I felt as if I was living on borrowed time. I didn't like the feeling.

Searching the ruined interior of the wreck, I was consumed with worry. We were in the middle of nowhere, with nothing but sand in all directions. There was no food and maybe enough water for six hours under the relentless sun. Worst of all, there was no means of communication! The antenna was buried under the wreck, and though I tried again and again to make contact over my radio with a medi-vac (emergency helicopter), it was no use. My pleas for help were not heard.

Nobody knew we existed. Even the boys at the base camp didn't expect us back for a whole day. There would be no search for at least that long. A helpless fear welled up inside me. I called for a medi-vac one last time. I waited. There was a terrible silence. We were alone! Fighting off despair, I grabbed my rifle, a box of ammo and a ragged blanket, and returned to Tony. The only thing left was faith, but I was losing even that. For me, there was no hope in sight.

Tony became more coherent and asked, "What the hell happened?"

I explained the accident, adding an apology at the end.

Tony raised his hands toward the sky. "You worry too much, Stevie-boy. Just get us the hell out of here!"

I smiled, and then lied straight into my friend's frightened eyes. "No sweat, boss. I made the call. Help should be here in no time."

Tony said nothing. He just grinned weakly as he lapsed back into unconsciousness. Rocking him back and forth, I looked over at the wreck. The hopelessness tore at my very core. Looking down at my older friend, I knew it was better that Tony didn't know the truth; a truth which meant probable death.

There was nothing I could do. We were both in rough shape. Traveling on foot was impossible. The radio was no longer an option. The only thing to do was wait. I hated that lack of control. As the steady breezes covered Tony and me with sand, I felt as if we were sitting in an hourglass with our time running out. With all Allied forces heading farther north, the chance of someone driving past were extremely remote. Situated somewhere on the southern tip of Iraq, we were in big trouble.

The two longest hours of my life passed without a change in our dilemma. With each passing minute, the outcome looked more bleak. Tony was in and out of consciousness. I sat alone, wincing from physical pain and struggling with mental torment. It was too much. My platoon sergeant was getting worse, and there was nothing more I could do. The trauma tore me apart. I feared Tony's death more than my own. For the first time during the war, I cried.

I sobbed in despair, even self-pity. Time crawled by, though it was irrelevant. Tony was dying from his physical wounds, and I was all but dead inside. I'd never felt so broken. I had never wanted to die alone. Then, I didn't have to.

An American vehicle appeared on the horizon. A miracle had been sent. The cavalry was on its way!

The hand of an angel rested upon my shoulder. Looking up, I stared into his face. A soldier bent down and gently whispered, "Lay down, Sarge. I'm gonna take care of you now. It's all over. We're gonna get you out of here." With that, he winked.

I couldn't believe it. It was the lost soldier I'd given directions to a few months before.

"But how did you...?" I started.

He smiled. "Nice to see you again, too. After the directions you gave me, I finally found my medical unit." He looked back at the road. "I'm assigned to the scout vehicle. I'm about ten minutes ahead of our convoy. They should be along in a bit."

"So how did you know we were here?" I asked. "Did you hear my radio transmission?" I knew the Hum-V's antenna was buried, but still, there was no other logical explanation for his sudden appearance. At that time, in that place, it would have been a miracle for anyone to happen by.

"What transmission?" he replied. "We were just passing through."

In disbelief, I collapsed onto the hot sand. My throbbing body could finally rest; my tortured mind was at ease.

Sergeant Jason Matthews, a medic, called for a chopper, and then worked feverishly over me. I was strapped to a long-board, while my pants and shoulder holster were completely cut off. My arm was splintered, and my neck placed into a bulky brace. An IV was administered, and through it all, I slipped in and out of the real world.

Tony was also shoved into a cocoon of precautionary devices, while an IV was stuck into his thirsty veins. After a few mumbled complaints, he fell asleep in the shadow of a praying army chaplain. I was relieved to find out that his condition was stable.

Before long, the medi-vac chopper flew in for the pick-up. After covering me from head to toe with a warm foil wrap, Sergeant Matthews placed his upper body over my face, shielding me from the blowing sand. Touching down, the airborne ambulance's motor was cut down to a high-pitched whine. It was the most welcome screech I had ever heard.

Four men lifted Tony up and rushed him toward the helicopter. Upon their return, the same men lifted up my canvas litter, and at a sprint, I was also rushed to the helicopter. Tony was fast asleep. Looking back at Matthews, I yelled, "Thank you," though there was no way he could have heard me. The chopper was too loud.

With a look of urgency, though, Matthews ran over to me. He grabbed my hand and placed something into the palm. With a wonderful smile, he threw a thumbs-up and was gone. I opened my hand. It was my gold wedding band, slightly misshapen, but shining brightly. Goose bumps raced over my body. It was too unbelievable to be real. Yet, it was true. I had lived through it. I slid the ring back onto my finger, and the chopper took to the air.

Miraculously, Tony and I both healed. I stayed in the Army until the Gulf War ended. Tony retired with a disability from the Army, and to this day, still offers to pay for driving lessons for me.

By Steve Manchester

Steven Manchester is the published author of *The Unexpected Storm: The Gulf War Legacy*; *Jacob Evans,* and *At The Stroke of Midnight,* as well as several books under the pen name, Steven Herberts. He has also written films that have been produced, including, *Acquaintances* and *Gooseberry Island.* When not spending time with his two sons, writing, or promoting his published books/films, this Massachusetts author speaks publicly to troubled school children through the "Straight Ahead" Program.

Fate on the Fly

The engraved invitation rests in a silver frame on my husband Dick's desk. The ink is fading after years of the Arizona sun beating on it through his office window.

> **The family of**
> **Mr. and Mrs. Donald E. Day request**
> **the pleasure of your company**
> **at a buffet dinner to celebrate**
> **the Fiftieth Anniversary of their marriage**
> **on Sunday, the sixteenth of August, at four o'clock**
> **at Westcourt in the Buttes**
> **2000 Westcourt Way, Tempe, Arizona**

The invitation arrived in the mail near the end of July 1987. Donald and Genevieve Day were the parents of our friends, brothers Don and Bill Day, and we were pleased that they were including us in their anniversary celebration. This was a party we did not want to miss. The problem was that Dick, the president of our family-owned company, planned to spend the week before the Days' party working in our Detroit office, and his parents were expecting him to stay on to visit them in Erie, Pennsylvania, over that weekend. Dick almost always visited his parents when he went to Detroit on business because his father was 88 years old, his mother 80, and he knew each visit with them could be the last.

Family members and friends were familiar with Dick's routine of winding up business trips to Detroit with a weekend visit to his parents' home in Erie, which was less than an hour away from Detroit by commuter airline. He would then normally take a late Sunday afternoon Northwest commuter flight from Erie back to Detroit in time to catch Northwest Airlines Flight 255, which left Detroit at 8:45 p.m. to fly non-stop to Phoenix.

This schedule allowed Dick to spend the most time with his parents, and with the time change, still get back to Phoenix at a reasonable hour. He always traveled by Northwest Airlines to get the mileage to qualify for their annual "Gold Card."

24

If Dick kept to his normal schedule, however, and returned to Phoenix on Northwest Airlines Flight 255 on the day of the Days' anniversary, he would miss the party, so he changed his reservations. He arranged to leave Erie on a morning commuter flight to Detroit, about five hours earlier than usual, and then caught an earlier Northwest flight from Detroit back to Phoenix.

Dick remembers his father saying to him when he dropped him off at the Erie Airport, "I wish you would stay longer, Richard," and his response, "I would, Dad, but we have this party in Arizona tonight."

Upon Dick's arrival home, I picked him up at Phoenix's Sky Harbor Airport, we drove directly to Westcourt in the Buttes, a beautiful resort, and we had a wonderful time partying with the Day family and friends until late that evening.

When we stepped into the kitchen upon our arrival home, the flashing light on the telephone answering machine caught our attention. To our bewilderment, the machine was loaded with frantic messages from family members and friends begging to know if Dick was safe and imploring us to return their calls when we got home, regardless of the hour.

With our first returned call, to our son Jim, we learned that Northwest Airlines Flight 255 had gone out of control during takeoff from the Wayne County Airport, smashed into a highway overpass, and exploded. We had not had occasion to tell most of our family members and friends that Dick was taking an earlier flight back to Phoenix that Sunday, and they assumed that, as usual, he was on Flight 255.

Described in later court proceedings as the "second-worst aviation disaster in American history," the crash killed 154 passengers and crew members (everyone on board, except one four-year old girl) and two people on the ground. Investigators concluded that the crash occurred because the pilot forgot to set wing flaps before takeoff.

If not for the Days having chosen August 16 as their wedding date fifty years earlier and inviting us to their party fifty years later, Dick would have been in the wrong place at the wrong time—aboard Northwest Flight 255—and I would have been a widow. It is as though Dick were supposed to die, and by pure chance (or *was it?*), something that happened 50 years earlier gave him a reason to change his plans, and saved his life.

Although the ink on the party invitation is fading with the passage of time, the emotional impact on me when I read it today is as powerful as it was when I looked at it, in awe, the day after the party.

By Brenda Warneka

Brenda Warneka is a partner in the law firm of Cox Warneka Redmon in Scottsdale, Arizona. She has a BA in history and is also a CPA. She usually writes on legal topics. She is a long time contributor of articles to *The Maricopa Lawyer* and a member of the Arizona Press Women. Brenda is married, with children, grandchildren, and two black standard poodles. She has a wide range of interests, including history, art, literature, theater, hiking, international travel, genealogy, and photography, and she and her husband, Dick, are long standing, charter members of a gourmet club, where he does the cooking.

Unlikely Bouquet

Fate is the sum total of all of the trivial events that you never thought would amount to anything and that will affect everything forever.

She stares out from the pages of her scrapbook, challenging me to unravel the story of her fate and mine. This album is no longer a mirror into which she peers to find her own youthful reflection. With the passage of time, it has become a fragile window in which I can vaguely see my own blurred image. I did not share in these memories. I struggle to decipher faces, gestures, and notes to trace how her life unfolded, seeking to unravel not just a story, but a person. My fate grew from hers, and without the exact sequence of events that the forces of youth, duty, love, and geology conspired to arrange, I would not be here today.

Youth

Barbara Nemanich. Her personal record begins near the end of her high school days. She pasted various scraps and mementos into her album: photographs, letters, valentines, news-clippings and handwritten notes. It is a collage of who she was then. She entitled this section "Funology," the word itself a newsprint cut-out.

The only pervasive theme or pattern throughout the album is her presence. In page after page, she smiles out crookedly, trying to conceal an overbite, head tilted slightly downward. Nameless friends swarm around her, clinging like insects, on the periphery of her story. In this space, she is the central character.

THE SENIOR CLASS PRESENTS
Green Stockings
By AEW Mason
Friday, April 23, 1924
Produced by special arrangement
with Samuel French of New York
Starring Barbara Nemanich as Madge (Mrs. Rockingham)

Dear Mr. Nemanich:

Your daughter, Barbara, will graduate next spring. She has done excellent work during her attendance at the Tower-Soudan High School.
We are highly pleased with her in every way.

Yours very truly, BFE, Principal H.S.

CLASS TO FINISH AT TOWER HIGH SCHOOL

Tower, Minn., June 6 (Special to *The Herald*): Graduation exercises for the Tower-Soudan High School will be held tonight at the school, when Dr. J. W. Holland of St. Paul will give the address. Musical numbers and other features have been arranged. Miss Hazel Johnson is the salutatorian and Miss Barbara Nemanich is the valedictorian.

Barbara enrolls in college, where perhaps she will continue her study of acting. Brochure pictures of vast dining halls and cloistered dorm rooms are affixed to the pages. The images are without a single student to disrupt the order of the chairs or scuff the gleaming floors. A pennant bearing the name Villa St. Scholastica, slashes its way across the adjacent page.

An unsigned note appears folded over, with simply, "I love you, Barbara," scrawled onto the torn sheet. She becomes engaged during her first year in college. Maybe he was one of the boys in a football uniform staring stoically outward in a photo, taken in front of the school, appearing as naively fearless as a young soldier preparing for war. But this future of continuing in school, of marrying this now nameless boy, was not to be hers.

Duty

The first page of the next section, entitled "Family," bears photographs of all her siblings. Each child has his or her own grouping of pictures trimmed down from larger photos into unlikely and odd shapes. Shards of each childhood hit the eyes like angles of a prism. Some of the photos are somber, Sunday-clothed and posed. Other glimpses are full of smiles and spirit. There are seven children, including herself—names scrawled by each grouping: Barbara, Victoria, George, John, Joseph, Agnes, and Rose. This family is the foundation upon which her identity was built and which almost consumed her entirely.

The next page bears the word MOTHER in iridescent foil lettering. Opposite this page is the picture of a tombstone, and a calendar noting the events that happened in swift succession in June and July of 1925.

June 13th: The day I came home for my summer vacation from the villa.

June 15th: The day Mother became ill.

June 26th: Mother's last days at home upon this earth. Mother left for Duluth (St. Mary's) at 7:30 a.m., never to return.

July 1st: Mother was operated on.

July 2nd: We all went to Duluth, for Mother was feeling worse.

July 3rd: Mother died at 8:30 am.

July 4th: Mother's body was shipped home.

July 5th: Mother's funeral.

Although, in the next pictures, Barbara continues to smile at the camera, the smile is somewhat more tentative. Certain hopes had been dashed. She would not return to school in the fall; she would stay at home to help her father raise the younger children. Instead of continuing as a scholar and an actress, within the course of a few weeks, she assumed the most serious and tragic role in her young life. Barbara at once had lost a mother and become a mother.

Time moved on. She continued to visit her friends at school, although she herself no longer attended. Instead of noting her own achievements, now she tracked the achievements of her friends. Her fiancé broke off the engagement because he would not wait for her indenture to her family to be fulfilled. Her world became smaller. She could only watch as her friends moved on.

During one of these unmarked days, Barbara was courted by another man. He did not appear in the pictures in front of the school. His name was not in the program of a play. And he did not ever wear a football uniform. He was one of the boys who had quit school early to become a lumberjack and a miner. Every day he descended deep into the underground mine that was the wellspring of the town. As a barman, his job was to take a heavy bar and chip loose rock from the ceiling of a newly formed cavern after a dynamite blast. He would be the first person in after the fumes dissipated and the dust settled. He ensured stability and safety for the rest of the crew that followed.

The rock that the mine produced was iron ore, which is enormously dense and strong. The make-up of the rock diminished the typical dangers associated with mining more porous rock, such as coal. Because of its density, the ore was relatively predictable; cave-ins almost never occurred. Silicosis did not plague the lungs. And the men emerged with red-dust clinging to their clothing and hair, instead of black.

As was his nature, Anthony was a silent man, and he made an entrance into her life quietly. He won her affection. He waited for her. When the younger children had grown to adolescence, Barbara looked forward to finally embarking on a married life of her own. She became engaged a second time. Wedding plans were made. Now, she would exchange her role as a mother for a role as a wife.

Love

Barbara's sister, Rose, was only a small girl of perhaps four in the opening pages of the scrapbook. She is the child who stands in front of their mother's knees, tendrils of hair falling down past her shoulders, a half-dozen roses bunched in her small hands, eyes staring blankly into the camera. Shortly before Barbara's wedding, Rose, who by now was 11 years old, was diagnosed with tuberculosis. Later, it would be discovered that Rose had contracted the disease from the school nurse, who for unknown reasons continued to stay in contact with the children at the school despite her illness.

Now, I peer through this window into the past and begin filling in the images that are absent on the later pages. I imagine Barbara in the kitchen, involved in some necessary chore, cooking or washing dishes. She is contemplating how she has come to this place in her life twice. Twice on the brink of marriage, and twice sickness and death have joined together to impede her path. As she stares out the kitchen window, a battle is being waged within her as she attempts to balance duty to family and allegiance to herself. When her mother died, she followed the demands of Duty and later lost Love because of it. It is less than a week before the ceremony is to take place and a decision regarding whether or not to proceed has to be made.

Ultimately, she has to make it. Would the dutiful action be to postpone the wedding? Would the selfish action be to proceed? She knows that Anthony will defer to her judgment. Despite the patience he has already exhibited, he will not deliver an ultimatum. However, the simple burden of having to make such a tradeoff is enough to crush her resolve; to cause her to postpone the ceremony to a later, happier day.

There is a knock at the door. Before she has a chance to remove her apron, her parish priest enters.

"Hello, Barbara."

"Hello, please, sit down," she says, somewhat flustered by his unexpected arrival.

"I've heard the news about Rose. Awful. How is she doing?"

"Her condition is serious. We've sent her to Duluth for confinement."

Barbara has attended mass every Sunday and also attends daily mass during the week. It is a purposeful ritual on her part. She feels validation for her own sacrifice, and the power of the social network embeds her to that purpose. The priest has seen her through the entire saga. He wonders how she is bearing the news. He sits at the kitchen table with her.

"Barbara, I know that you must be considering canceling the wedding."

She looks down at the towel still in her hands. She cannot bear to reveal the turmoil that races within her.

"I am here to encourage you to go through with it, just as planned. I am here to tell you that this is what God would want. God has brought you and Tony together for a reason. And God wants to see you happy."

She nods, and her shoulders drop with relief that a decision has been made.

And here is the wedding picture. Both Barbara and Anthony are posed and somber. She holds an unlikely bouquet of white lilies. A long, flowing gown drapes to the floor. He stares squarely ahead and beyond the camera.

Rose would eventually recover from her illness, but the tradeoff of a life was made that day.

Geology

Although it was an uncommon event, the man who took Anthony's place in the mine, during his wedding, was killed in an accident. Every night, the enormous chamber that Anthony was assigned to was enlarged by blasting outward and upward until the ceiling came within close proximity to the floor of the mined-out chamber above.

As the wedding photograph was being taken, Anthony's replacement entered the mine chamber after waiting for the dust to settle after a blast. He then proceeded to carefully chip away at the small loose pieces of rock still embedded in the ceiling. What he could not have known was that some of those pieces were precariously holding a massive load of rock in place above his head. The circumstance was created thousands of years earlier when glaciers deposited sediment in this exact, but faulty, strata. The motion of weather and earth combined to create a less than uniform layer of rock.

The result was that the unfortunate barman was crushed and killed on Barbara and Anthony's wedding day. Had Anthony not been married on that day, he would have been performing the same work in the same chamber and would have been killed in the accident that was thousands of years in the making.

If Barbara had married her previous fiancé, Anthony would have died. If she simply had stayed in school and continued to pursue drama, he would have died.

If she had not agreed to marry him, he would have died. Perhaps she might have cut the news from the paper and pasted it into her album, a sad memorial to a boy from her hometown.

For me, this is the story about how my grandparents came together. I have been told that I have inherited Barbara's eyes and the bridge of her nose. In my own memory of her, I can only envision the tint of her hair, the shape of her eyeglasses, the spots on her hands, the vague smell of powder that always engulfed her. She died when I was five. But all I really have to do is look into the mirror to see her staring back. Part of her has been preserved in me. Some small evidence of immortality. She always said that she saved her husband's life by marrying him. In this way, she will remain at the center of my story forever.

By Terese Yapel

Terese Yapel grew up in Minnesota where she learned the value of a good novel on a cold winter afternoon. Her current interests include drinking coffee and dreaming about potential travel destinations (although she travels far less than she should). Knowing this, she aspires to learn Italian during her various and frequent commutes from Marin County to San Francisco to Sonoma County (and to spill less coffee along the way). Terese is currently pursuing her MFA in Creative Writing at the University of San Francisco.

We All Cross Paths for a Reason

My good friend, Cynthia Adams, was a career nurse who came from a long line of nurses. Nursing in her family was like a genetic predisposition. Her mother, her grandmother and her great grandmother had all been nurses. And, although Cynthia was adopted at birth, she reasoned that she had received the "nursing gene" through association at an early age.

Cynthia's adoptive father abandoned them when she was young, but her adoptive mother more than made up for his absence, raising Cynthia as her own flesh and blood, never making excuses for her adoptive father's failings. Cynthia went on to graduate from high school and nursing school and then became one of the best nurses ever employed at Branson Memorial.

Cynthia was writing notes on a patient's chart when she heard the radio behind her. It squealed, popped off a series of low tones and then squealed again. The desk nurse, Ruby Smith, picked up the microphone and answered the call.

"We have a vehicle collision," the paramedic on the other end of the radio reported. "Three injuries; transporting two your way."

"Transport time?" Ruby asked.

"Ten minutes tops," the paramedic answered. "We have one in critical condition."

At the word "critical," Cynthia felt her stomach lurch forward, then settle back again.

Cynthia waited while Ruby finished some paperwork. She looked at the wall clock, 11:55 p.m.—her shift ended in five minutes. Another check-in wouldn't take that much time and then it was home to a nice warm bed.

"I'll take this one, Ru," Cynthia said, grabbing a pair of latex gloves.

"Are you sure?" Ruby asked.

"Yep, but after that, I'm gone."

There had been an automobile accident. Two drunken teens ran a red light, plowing into the car of Mr. and Mrs. Joshua Banks. The first ambulance arrived with Mr. Banks, an eighty-three-year old white male, who was suffering from a head injury, with an indication of massive internal and external injuries. Cynthia watched as the paramedics carried him on a gurney down the hallway and disappeared. A police officer recounted what had happened at the scene to other emergency room staff, as the second ambulance arrived.

Anita Banks, a seventy-nine-year old white female, had a broken arm, but other than that, appeared to have come through the accident relatively unscathed. When the ambulance doors were thrown open, Cynthia saw concern on the older woman's face, and realized that she had no idea what her husband's condition might be.

"Where is Joshua?" Mrs. Banks asked as the paramedics pulled the mobile gurney from the vehicle. Cynthia didn't speak, but attempted to start the vital-sign readings. She studied her patient quickly. Mrs. Banks wore expensive clothes. It was obvious that she was well-to-do.

"The doctors are taking care of him," Cynthia said.

"Look, young lady, I'm all right," Mrs. Banks said firmly. "But I need to know how my husband is. Either you answer my questions, or I'll go find out myself."

"I understand your concern, Mrs. Banks," Cynthia said softly. "If you will cooperate with me, I'll find out what I can about your husband."

"Be quick about it!" exclaimed Mrs. Banks.

Cynthia watched the woman as she checked her blood pressure and temperature. She wore her gray hair pulled back, out of her face, with just a hint of bang on the right side of her forehead. Her face, although stern, had soft lines around the eyes.

"What's your first name, ma'am?" Cynthia asked. She was concerned about Mrs. Banks' blood pressure, which was sky-high; she had to calm her down. Cynthia glanced at the clock, 12:13 a.m.

"Anita," the woman answered. "My friends call me Nita."

"Well, which would you prefer that I call you?" Anita Banks seemed surprised at the question, but pleased. Her body relaxed a little, and the lines in her forehead relaxed.

"Nita, please."

"Okay, Nita, now I need you to try and calm down. Can you do that?"

Nita looked perplexed. "But my husband..." she started.

Cynthia put up a hand to stop any further protest.

"Nita, which hospital did you say you worked for?"

"I don't," Nita said, confused.

"Then your husband is probably in better hands than yours right now, right?" Cynthia smiled to ease the tension. The older woman considered for a moment, and then sighed, her shoulders conceding to Cynthia's logic.

"I suppose you're right," she said. "It's our anniversary, and I just, well, I just…I don't know what I'd do without him."

Cynthia touched Nita's shoulder softly. "He's in good hands, Nita."

"Thank you." Cynthia looked at the clock again, 12:17 a.m. She should be well on her way home by now.

"Will you stay with me for a while?" Nita asked quietly.

Cynthia considered for a moment. She really needed to go home and get some sleep. But, she looked at Nita again and decided to stay a while longer. Heck, what could it hurt?

"I'll stay," she said carefully. "But let me go check on Mr. Banks first."

"Joshua, please; he hates to be called Mr. Banks."

"Okay," Cynthia said, smiling. She left the room and walked to the desk.

"You're supposed to be gone," Ruby said.

"I know, but Mrs. Banks asked if I'd stay a little while, and she's so scared for her husband, I figured, why not?"

"You're a glutton for punishment," Ruby said, shaking her head.

"How is her husband?" Cynthia asked, reaching for his chart. She hesitated before looking at it.

"Not good," Ruby answered grimly.

Cynthia glanced over the chart and then returned it to the desk. Mr. Banks had massive internal injuries, and the doctors were having a hard time stopping the bleeding.

"Could you call me if there's any news?" Cynthia asked.

"Sure thing," Ruby answered.

When Cynthia returned to Nita's room, she pulled up a chair close to the bed. Nita settled into the bed a little. Cynthia wasn't sure that her staying was going to mean much, but her misgivings disappeared with the look of relief that appeared on the elderly woman's face.

"How long have you been married?" asked Cynthia.

"Sixty years," Nita stated quietly. "Sixty years of love and companionship that I couldn't have gotten from anyone else."

"Sounds like you love him a great deal."

"Yes, we've had a wonderful marriage. We are very lucky."

"Yes, you are," reflected Cynthia, thinking about the confrontations between her mother and father, before he walked out of their lives. Why couldn't *her* parents have been like that? Why couldn't she have been the child of people like these? Cynthia reached out and took Nita's hand. Nita squeezed her hand back with a warm, knowing smile. She looked deeply into Cynthia's eyes, and, suddenly, Cynthia felt her soul lay bare and open.

"It will happen that way for you, too, one day," Nita said. She had noticed that Cynthia wore no wedding band. "You're a good person and nice things happen to good people."

"I don't think so, Nita; the women in my family don't have such great luck with men," Cynthia offered.

"We often have a way of making our own luck—or fate does it for us," Nita said, with a far-away look in her eyes. "I had a little girl once…"

"What happened?" Cynthia asked.

"We were young, and Joshua was off in the war. My own mother advised me against keeping the baby, even though Joshua and I were married, and it was all legal. I was ill and afraid, but I was determined to keep her; then I got word that Joshua had been killed in action. Thank God, it wasn't true, but, at the time, I didn't know that. I gave up my baby. I've never, for one day, stopped thinking about her. Joshua ended up running a very large company on the East Coast, but we never had any other children. We don't have children or grandchildren."

"I am adopted," Cynthia said thoughtfully. "I wish I had known my birth mother and father." They sat in comfortable silence for several minutes. Cynthia was about to say something when the door behind her opened, and a young doctor came in.

"Mrs. Banks?" the doctor said with a smile. "I'm Rory Telis, the on-call doctor. Your husband is in stable condition now."

Both Nita and Cynthia let out a relieved sigh and hugged one another.

"He has a skull fracture and some internal injuries, so we'll continue to watch him, but I believe he's going to be okay."

The doctor left, and Cynthia stood up. "I guess I'll go now," she said.

"Thank you. You have been really wonderful to stay here with me," Nita said, squeezing Cynthia's hand again.

"You're welcome. Thank you, Nita, for allowing me to get to know you."

"Well, that's what it's all about," said Nita. "We all cross paths for a reason. You never know what you take from a casual conversation with a stranger."

They both smiled, and Cynthia went to the nurses' station to complete the paperwork for the Banks.

"Where are their personal effects?" Cynthia asked Ruby. Ruby pulled a basket out from under the back counter. Cynthia sat down and dumped the contents onto the counter top. It was the responsibility of the closing nurse to bag and tag the patients' effects. She knew Ruby would do it, but for some reason, she felt compelled to do it herself.

She tagged Nita's things first. A purse, small, but in good taste, contained the usual lipstick and compact. There was a wallet, tan leather with contrasting trim. She opened the wallet because any money had to be counted. She counted $11.38 and logged it onto the list. She was about to put the wallet in the bag when a photograph caught her eye. She took a closer look and felt tears well up as she realized that it was an old picture of Nita and Joshua. She folded the wallet over and started to place it in the bag when something fell out. It was another photo.

"Darn!" she whispered. She hated feeling like she was snooping. She picked it up and started to put it back in the wallet when handwriting on the back of the small picture caught her attention.

"My daughter Taby," the photo read. Cynthia flipped it over. A gasp caught in her throat. Dropping the photo onto the table top, she reached under the cabinet and brought out her purse. Digging into the purse as if in desperation, she located her wallet and threw it open to her own photos. There, on top, was a photo of her as a newborn. It was one her mother had said her birth mother had given to them; it was identical to the picture from Nita's wallet.

Cynthia stood up and walked to the door of Room 298. Nita was sitting in bed, staring out the window. Cynthia heard Nita's words again: "We all cross paths for a reason."

"Mother!" Cynthia choked out.

Nita turned and smiled curiously as Cynthia reached for her hand.

By Jamie D'Antoni

Postscript: Cynthia says that finding each other was a Godsend because Nita had always wanted a child and grandchildren. She now has both.

Jamie D'Antoni is the author of three novels, *Beyond the Call*, *Deceptions* and *Grayson's Ransom*. In addition, she is Managing Editor and co-owner of a weekly newspaper on the coast of Washington State. She has been a journalist for over 16 years and free-lances for publications throughout the world. She also conducts a writers' workshop on "creative inspiration" at many writers' conferences. Jamie currently lives on the Washington coast with her partner, Mary Laws, and their sons, Aaron Kasper and Ryan Moore.

Time for Life

Fate is a train roaring down the track of life. Sometimes you step off the track, and unless you look back over your shoulder and see the train go roaring past, you don't know what you missed.

—Brenda Warneka

The Great Western Express was running its usual route to central London through Reading, Southall, Hanwell, and Ealing, terminating at Paddington Station. Commuters from the West Country relied on the fast train to reach the hub of England's metropolis.

It was 7:25 on a cool autumn morning. Alison prepared to leave for work. She and her children, Thomas and Madeleine, lived in a modest attached house with a small garden—delightfully called a "terraced house" in England. Only two weeks earlier, Alison had begun a new job as secretary for the legal director of a real estate agency in Nottinghill Gate, a prestigious, trendy part of London. This was the first job that she had had that gave her financial peace of mind. For the last ten years, she had struggled as a single parent to make ends meet by doing part-time hospital and secretarial work in her hometown of Ealing. Now, she was working in posh central London, making almost three times as much money, and she could hardly believe her good luck!

Delayed while preparing the children for school, Alison hurried to catch the train at the West Ealing railway station, just a ten-minute walk from home.

Alison's nephew, Adam, her brother John's son, frequently took the same train to work from Reading, about fifty miles west of London. A cool dude and an accomplished musician, Adam had graduated from Brighton College that summer and quickly obtained a lucrative position as program developer, part of a think-tank for a new television channel, Basil TV Productions. Well on his way to a successful career, he was full of enthusiasm for his new prospects.

Alison dashed up Manor Road past the shops, over the bridge that crossed the railway lines, and along the other side. Approaching the station house, she looked beyond it toward the railway platform. Suddenly, the expression on her face turned to dismay. There was her train pulling away from West Ealing, picking up speed. She watched in disbelief, as it zoomed off into the distance toward Paddington. "Damn! I'll be late for work," she muttered. A few other frustrated commuters missed the train, too. They would all have to wait for the next one.

They waited, but the next train did not come. A short while later, there was an announcement on the platform loudspeaker. There would be no more trains into the city that morning. Commuters would have to go to Ealing Broadway and catch the tube on the underground Central Line. They could take the bus to the subway station, but it was rush hour, and a brisk twenty-minute walk would get them there more quickly.

Now it was clear that Alison would be very late for work, and she began to worry. How could she have been so stupidly, haplessly late for the train when she had just started such a fine job and was desperately trying to make a good impression on her boss? Before catching the tube at Ealing Broadway, she had to find a telephone to let the office know she was on her way.

An hour earlier in Reading, Adam left home to catch the Great Western Express. As he approached the station, he glanced at his watch, and a glint of copper caught his eye. There on the sidewalk lay a penny, shining up at him, beckoning. "A lucky penny!" he fancied as he reached down to pick it up. Happily, he dropped it into his pocket and continued toward the station.

When Adam arrived, the train was already there. He strode across the platform to one of the carriages and grabbed the handle to open the door. As his fingers closed around the metal grip, the train's electronic, automatic locking system engaged. The doors of every car were locked instantly. "This can't be happening!" he thought, but there was nothing at all that he could do. He worked the handle two or three times in vain, and then turned on his heels, furious with himself. Had he arrived a moment earlier, he would have been on his way to London.

The time he had taken to pick up that "lucky" penny had caused him to miss his train. He reached into his pocket and flung the penny across the platform with contempt. Now he would have to wait for the next train, and he would be late for work.

At 8:30, Adam's father John, a retired hydraulics engineer, turned on the television at home in Reading to watch the morning news. Suddenly, his face turned ashen.

The BBC was reporting breaking news of what would soon be known as the most disastrous train crash in the United Kingdom for forty-two years. On October 5, 1999, as the Great Western Express approached Paddington on one of the busiest sections of Britain's railway network, the westbound Thames train was leaving the terminal. It turned off a minor outbound line to continue onto a faster track, maneuvering across the inbound line traveled by the Great Western. The red stoplight was lit, but the Thames train did not heed the signal. And horror of horrors! The Great Western Express crashed head-on into the Thames train, causing explosions, fire, chaos, and destruction. Many passengers were trapped behind the electronically locked doors of the train. At least 70 people were killed and 150 injured.

"Adam! He was on that train. Oh dear God!" Uncontrolled fear seared through John's veins. "And Alison! What about Alison?" He was trembling, nearly crazed with panic. "This can't be! No, this can't be happening to my family!"

And it wasn't. What caused Alison to be just a few minutes late for the train when she was so eager to reach her new job on time? What made Adam stop for an insignificant piece of copper discarded on the sidewalk? Fate had worked its magic on this favored family saying, "Live on!"

When Alison heard about the train crash, she felt protected and blessed. Adam realized that he had indeed picked up a very lucky penny. Later that month, when the family celebrated John's sixty-first birthday, they looked into each other's eyes and knew that good fortune was surely theirs.

By Jill Ronsley

Jill Ronsley is a free-lance writer and copy editor. She has published articles in magazines and on web sites, and she has edited books and various works by different authors. Her writing interests include travel, culture, philosophy and meditation in India, human interest essays, children's stories, and articles on English language and style. She has a BA from McGill University. For more information about her work, visit www.suneditwrite.com.

What Is Fate?

I believe that almost all significant things are controlled by fate. What family we are born into. What genes we are born with. Whether we are black, white, red or yellow. What preferences we have. If we cross the street at four o'clock and find a winning lottery ticket lying in the gutter. If we cross that same street an hour later and get hit by a car. Some things we can control, mainly attitude, resolve and our power to reason. Other than those, and some of the positives or negatives stemming from them, I say it's all up to fate. Or maybe what I'm really saying is it's all up to Whoever created this world and controls it.

Jerry Bower (writer, farmer, adventurer)

Go Home

There's a divinity that shapes our ends, rough-hew them how we will.

—William Shakespeare.

The day Grandma died was my eighth birthday. My best gift was a game board with numbers and letters printed on it. It was rough—handmade and hand painted, with a pointer mounted on castors, which was used to spell out messages from "spirits." There was no card, and the wrappings looked used. When no one owned up to giving it to me, Mama grabbed it off the dining room table, and threw it into the trash. "It's superstitious nonsense—that silly spirit board. Devil worship," she said. "It's not for you." I fished it out of the trash can after dinner when she wasn't looking. It was mine, and I wanted it.

I thought Grandma didn't know it was my birthday. She had been curled up in her big oak bed since Christmas. The cancer started on her face and shoulders where years of farm work had left her skin mottled and wrinkled. In December, the doctor told Mama that he could order chemotherapy, but it would not help. In the end, she would still die a painful death. "No, we'll take her home and let her die in her own bed," Mama said.

So, we spent the winter, and on into the spring, at Grandma's house in West Virginia, watching her waste away. At first, Grandma spent part of the day in a wooden rocker, with a ragged cushion, telling me stories and braiding my hair. But, toward the end of May, she stopped getting out of bed, and you could hear her moaning and talking to herself from the kitchen. As the summer wore on, Grandma forgot who I was.

"Sister, have you fed the chickens?" she would say to me. "How many times do I have to ask you to feed the chickens?"

"Grandma, there are no chickens, and I'm not Sister."

"Sister, don't argue. Do what I tell you."

Air doesn't move in a dying person's room. Even the breeze would rather be someplace else.

"You sit there and watch her. If she needs me, call," Mama ordered. Grandma gasped for breath, shuddering and rasping.

I rocked back and forth in the rocking chair beside her bed, and prayed to God and Grandma, "Don't let me be sitting here by myself when it happens."

It was especially stifling after my birthday party. While Mama was cleaning up, I was watching Grandma. She stirred a little and opened her eyes.

"Sister, did you get my present?" She stared at me. "It was for you."

"What present?"

"You know. Your birthday present. I love you, Sister. Now, go home."

Grandma sank back and her mouth fell open.

"Mama! Quick! Hurry, Mama, Mama!"

As soon as Mama came, I ran to my room, which was directly above Grandma's room. The cicadas, the pear tree and the crying from Grandma's room below made me sick.

I picked up my spirit board and balanced it lightly on my knees. Tuning out everything, I listened only to the noises in my head while my fingers spelled the words, "GO HOME. GO HOME. GO HOME."

The burial was over in short order, and now I could hear voices from the room below as Mama divided up Grandma's possessions. "It was a blessing. She was in such pain." "Thank God she didn't know anything or anybody at the end." "She was a good woman. She worked so hard all of her life."

Through it all, the spirit board kept telling me: "GO HOME, GO HOME, GO HOME."

"We'll go when we can," Mama was telling someone. "This kind of business takes time."

But, the spirit board didn't listen. "GO HOME."

"I thought I threw that thing away." Mama appeared at my door as the message came through one more time. "You're too old and too smart for that kind of trash. Get rid of it!"

"No!"

"Don't be smart with me, young lady. You're being disrespectful. Your grandmother would never have put up with it. Now, let me have that thing."

"No. It's mine. Grandma gave it to me."

"Your grandmother did no such thing, but I don't have time to argue with you. Just throw it away, and we'll forget this happened."

"I want to go home. I want to leave here," I sobbed.

"Tomorrow. We're going tomorrow. But, don't try to bring that thing, or I'll give you something to cry about!"

The spirit board was adamant, "GO HOME." I loaded my things into the car and when Mama wasn't looking, I stuffed "Spirit" out of sight under the back of the driver's seat. It was nearly noon when we left. The car swayed around the mountains. The spirit board slipped out from under its hiding place. I dived to get it. "Don't kick the back of my seat. You're too old for that."

It was rainy, and the roads were slick. Mama didn't even turn around as she yelled at me. I rested the board on my knees and waited for the message, "GO HOME."

"I'm putting an end to this once and for all. Spirit boards are for pagan, stupid people." Mama reached behind her, grabbed the board and heaved it out the car window. It landed in somebody's cornfield. I watched through the back window, trying to count the rows.

Mama's neck was red. "We usually stop and get ice cream. But today, after this spirit board business, I don't think that's a good idea. We're going straight home. No stops; no treats."

She aimed the car across the bridge over the Ohio River. The four o'clock whistle blew, announcing shift change as we passed. Not stopping for ice cream kept us ahead of the coal mine traffic, which usually meant the cars on the bridge were bumper to bumper. Today, we were practically alone.

"I'll bet you're hungry," Mama said, a few miles past the bridge. "We would have stopped if you hadn't insisted on bringing that stupid board. Now you'll just have to wait."

"Grandma gave me the spirit board. She wanted me to have it."

The car veered onto the shoulder as Mama turned around enough to slap my face.

I didn't cry. I just wanted to go home.

"I'm sorry, child, but you try my patience. Maybe I should stop and get a cup of coffee. I didn't mean to hurt you."

"I want to go home."

We stopped at a little roadside cafe. The owner had the radio on. The announcer was giving the horrendous details. Some people were crying. The bridge over the Ohio River had collapsed—only minutes after we crossed. Cars bumper to bumper at shift change all fell into the river, sliding unstoppable into the deep, churning water; 88 cars; 120 dead; 2 survivors.

Mama prayed for the dead. I prayed for Grandma and my spirit board.

By Jennie L. Phipps

Jennie L. Phipps is a business writer who specializes in media, small business and health. She's a regular contributor to *Newsweek Japan, Television Week, Bankrate.com, Industry Week* and *Investor's Business Daily,* as well as *Health Scout*

News and *Modern Physician.* She's passionate about old houses and writes about them for *Old-House Journal, Preservation Online,* and *Smart Homeowner.* Jennie also publishes a subscription newsletter, *Freelance Success* www.freelancesuccess.com, for professional nonfiction writers.

921 Earthquake: It Could Have Been Us

Fate is the ineluctable, life-altering events that happen to us in spite of our plans.

"But I already paid for two bus tickets to Nantou for tomorrow." I rolled away from Tom and punched my pillow in frustration. Tour book phrases—"peaceful beauty," "most serene unspoiled site," "refreshing walks among bamboo"—extolling Nantou, located in the center of Taiwan, surfaced in my mind.

"It can't be helped," my husband said. "The customer agreed to try our experimental product this weekend, and I'm the only one who can…"

I'd heard it all before. This wasn't the first time we'd ditched sightseeing excursions due to Tom's exemplary work ethic.

The next night, September 21st, 1999, instead of sleeping in a hotel in Nantou, we slept in our own bed in Kaohsiung. Falling asleep in a pique wasn't easy, but eventually I drifted off.

It was around 2:00 a.m. Our bed, our bedroom, the whole apartment, the entire thirteen-story building jerked back and forth. Doors creaked. Houseplants wobbled. Furniture tried to "walk" away. Water sloshed in the toilet bowls. A large mirror shattered: reflective shards sailed across the room. The motion reminded me of "riddling coal ashes" where you yank a coal stove grate back and forth to sift ashes from coal embers.

Having lived in Kaohsiung, Taiwan, for two and a half years, Tom and I were accustomed to earthquake temblors. Sometimes the tectonic movements felt good and lulled us into the fantasy of Mother Nature rock-a-bye-babying a giant cradle. But we knew. This time it was different.

Groggily, Tom asked, "Is this…?"

"Yes," I said.

We scampered out of bed and held onto each other in the doorway, for doorways and pillars are said to be points of strength in buildings. The procedure was repeated five or six more times during the night. At dawn, we learned from CNN what had happened. Cameras panned a Taipei hotel leaning drunkenly against an adjacent building. Down here in southern Taiwan, we went about the rest of Tuesday as usual. I don't think the fact that the city of Kaohsiung (which is as far south from the epicenter as Taipei is north) was unharmed was pointed out in the American newscasts. This quirk of fate, however, dominates my thoughts and prayers of gratitude.

In the past, when natural or man-made disasters struck somewhere, Turkey, Kobe, Kosovo, Chernobyl, I punched the remote if satellited images of despair bummed me out too much. Newscasts, beamed from some foreign country across the globe, can never totally impart a palpable sense of tragedy. However, living only miles away from villages, towns and cities pulverized by violent seismic activity made sticking my head in the sand impossible.

The aftermath of the 921 earthquake, as the Taiwanese dubbed it, seeped into our daily lives like dust settling down, inserting its presence in our routine. It wasn't until after CNN reporters reduced, and eventually quit, coverage of the quake that the scope of the damage became known, bit by bit. It was then that we learned through the local news media and from friends what the true impact was.

For example, en route to a luncheon, we came across a traffic jam at Kaohsiung City Hall caused by legions of civil servants and civilians loading trucks with clothing, tents, blankets, water, generators, diapers, rice and other supplies headed for areas that were likened to war zones.

On the fourth night of their entrapment, the younger of two brothers had a fateful dream about a hole in the wall behind their refrigerator, and that is, in fact, where they found an exit through the rubble and into daylight 130 hours after their building had fallen down around them.

Children learned that they were orphans. Thankfully, more than enough families were willing to welcome them into their homes.

Mountains forming the spine of the island shape-shifted. In the time it takes to sneeze, immense landslides re-routed rivers and created new lakes. Villages were buried under tons of earth and rock. Geology in action.

My husband and his buddy were eating noodles at a stall they frequent. The proprietor thanked Tom profusely for the success of an American rescue team. As the proprietor filled their bowls with free noodle soup, Tom's eyes filled with empathy and humility. "Thank you, thank you," he said quietly, "but it wasn't me. I didn't do anything." Later, he stood in a queue in order to donate clothing and money.

Six days after the quake, Tom and I were dining at our favorite restaurant. The two TVs on the wall glimmered with live shots of twisted re-bar, broken concrete, bridges and roads rumpled like throw rugs, and injured people. It was as if we were ingesting grief.

The quake occurred three days before the Mid-Autumn Moon Festival, a holiday akin to American Thanksgiving, so photos of ruins aglow with moonlight were especially poignant during the time when people should have been celebrating the holiday with family, not zipping them in body bags.

For months after the 921 earthquake struck, Taiwan was reminded not 1,000 times a year, but 1,000 times a day, of her unstable position in geology's workshop, for that is how many aftershocks emanated from the epicenters. Seismographic maps depict numerous epicenters speckling the entire island and several fault lines slashing across it. Down here in the south, the tremors, weakened by distance, caused mild dizziness. The stronger aftershocks—4.5, 4.8, 5.3, 6.8—filled me with dread. That Kaohsiung remained undamaged is miraculous. Then again, it's probably only a matter of time before Kaohsiung is shaken.

Since I'd experienced from a closer perspective how devastating earthquakes are, each of the aftershocks seemed longer, much longer than they actually were. "Stop, stop. I'm tired of this," I complained aloud, feeling more scared than I remember ever feeling. But the shaking continued. Then I thought of those people whose homes "pancaked" (flattened), of the survivors who hadn't bathed for weeks, of the 13-day-old infant and her 87-year-old grandma who were the sole survivors in their family, of the mass Buddhist funerals with the deceaseds' portraits and "Hello Kitty" toys arranged amid incense and orchids, and of the physical and psychological wounds.

As for me, it wasn't the initial quake that disturbed me. It was the cumulative effects of the aftermath that caused me to feel frightened, sad, awed, angry, inspired, and fortunate that the epicenter was in Nantou. If not for my husband's strong work ethic, I'd be telling a different story—or I might not be around to tell any story at all. We are so lucky.

By Beth Fowler

Beth Fowler is an American writer who has lived in Malaysia, England, Taiwan and Australia and has traveled extensively. In addition to being a free-lance author, who has had hundreds of articles and short stories published, Ms. Fowler has held jobs ranging from state park janitor to English teacher. She is the author of six books, including her latest novel, *The Dressmaker's Dummy*. You can find her at www.authorsden.com/bethfowler.

"Honor, Courage, and Commitment": Saving Jack Roush

The small open-cockpit Air-Cam lifted off the end of the runway at the Troy Municipal Airport, in Troy, Alabama, banked to the left, and flew along the shore of Palos Verdes Lake. The pilot undoubtedly was enjoying the view of the community of homes clustered around the tranquil body of water below. Set in the middle of scenic woodlands, the private man-made lake is about a mile long and ranges from 30 feet deep at one end to three feet deep at the other.

High-tension power lines on each side of the lake, partially obscured by trees, were hard to detect in the early evening light.

Without warning, disaster struck, as the twin-engine plane collided with steel cable support wires for the power line towers, and plunged, upside down, toward the lake, crashing into water that was about eight feet deep. The plane was mostly submerged as it settled in place.

Friday night, April 19, 2002, Larry and Donna Hicks were preparing to watch the six o' clock news at their lakeside home at Palos Verdes Estates, outside Troy. Hicks, a 52-year-old retired Sergeant Major with the Marines, worked as a conservation enforcement officer for the state of Alabama, and was in the last three weeks of studying for his Master's Degree in Law Enforcement at Troy State University. He had arrived home from work half an hour earlier, and he and Donna had talked about going to a movie, but decided against it.

The TV news was just starting when they looked out the window and saw a small plane flying down the shoreline of the lake. Donna commented on how pretty it was.

"I wonder if he knows about the power lines," Larry said, just as the aircraft suddenly shuddered to a halt, flipped over, and headed 80 to 100 feet straight down into Palos Verdes Lake. Hicks was already running out the back door, his heart racing, as the plane hit the water, yelling behind to his wife, "Call 911! I'm going to see if I can help the pilot."

49

Fortunately, Larry's brother, Wayne, had left a 14-foot aluminum johnboat, with an electric trolling motor, at the lake in preparation for bass fishing that day, then hadn't shown up. The boat was charged, with everything hooked up, ready to go. Donna made the call to 911, and ran outside in time to see Larry commandeering the johnboat, headed toward the Air-Cam, which was about 100 yards off shore.

When Hicks was stationed at the Marine Air Corps Station in Iwakuni, Japan, in 1984, he had spent two-and-a-half months, part time, in an intense Search and Rescue program. A Major Stone, who ran the SAR team, got him into it because he thought Hicks would be good at search and rescue since he was muscular and a body builder. The training was specifically directed toward saving pilots who had gone down in water in fixed-wing or rotary-wing planes. Hicks learned how to get pilots out from under canopies (parachutes) and helicopters, and out of planes that had crashed upside down. After the training, Major Stone asked Headquarters to transfer Hicks to the SAR team, but the telecommunications unit could not spare him. Hicks had never had the opportunity to use his specialized training.

The engines of the Air-Cam were hot when it hit Palos Verdes Lake, and the airplane was smoking in the water. High octane aviation fuel, from a ruptured fuel tank, floated over the surface in greasy patterns. The back half of the aircraft and a broken wing were sticking up from the water. Hicks climbed out of the boat onto the wing and tethered a line to the plane to keep the boat from floating away.

The harsh smell of gasoline assaulted his nostrils as Hicks turned and shouted at his wife before diving into the water, "Donna, no matter what happens, I love you!" Donna got out a puzzled, "What?" before she, too, smelled the gas. It was only later that Hicks thought about the danger of the plane blowing up.

The water was murky from mud kicked up when the plane hit the bottom of the lake, and Hicks had trouble getting his bearings underwater. The plane had crashed into the middle of an underwater "stump field," but luckily had missed hitting any trees. The first time down, Hicks felt only an empty seat and thought the pilot might have been thrown out of the plane; running out of air, he was forced to come back to the surface. It occurred to him that maybe the plane was a two-seater.

The second time down, just as he started to push off to go back up, he felt the back of a man's neck under his hand. The pilot was hanging upside down, still strapped into his harness. Hicks thought to himself, *Okay, now I know where he is.* Then, his SAR training kicked in. He came back to the surface, took a deep breath, and went down for the third time.

The pilot's face was so badly swollen when Hicks first saw him that his features were almost non-existent. The doctor later said this might have been because he was upside down and had a closed-head injury.

Larry's military training—the repeat drill of what to do until it became second nature—took over: "Locate Pilot, Extract Pilot..." Hicks felt for the pilot's seatbelt; fortunately, it was one he recognized by feel from his training in the military. He released the belt, and the pilot floated into his arms. Hicks swam to the surface, pulling the man with him. The pilot had bones sticking out through his legs, and his feet were turned the wrong way.

The man was bleeding through the nose and mouth, and was no longer breathing; he had drowned. The Troy police had arrived on the lake bank by now. Larry yelled to the officers, "He's not breathing," and he heard one police officer say to another, "He's dead."

Hicks hauled the man up against the wing that was sticking up above the water, put a modified Heimlich maneuver under his ribs, pulled up to get the water out of his lungs, and then started modified CPR. The inert figure coughed up water and blood; then on the fifth breath, started to breathe. "I've got him breathing again!" Hicks yelled to the rescue unit on the shore.

He gripped the wing of the plane with his left hand, lying on his back in the water, supporting the pilot on his chest with his right arm to keep his head above water. He was in the lake like this for about 15 minutes, waiting for help to arrive. The first five minutes, he felt a stinging sensation from the aviation fuel; the next five minutes were worse. At the end, he was in great pain. He found out later, the top layer of his skin had burned off.

The rescue unit brought out an extra boat, put the pilot on the backboard and floated him to shore; Larry warned them the man was too badly injured to put him in the boat. The four members of the rescue team walked out of the lake. Larry made it as far as the bank when his legs gave way. A recovering cancer victim, he had been taking shots to boost his energy, but a policeman had to help him out of the water. It was at that point that an Emergency Medical Technician told him that the pilot was Jack Roush. "Who is Jack Roush?" Larry asked. The police officer and the EMT laughed.

Hicks and the pilot were transported in different ambulances to Edge Regional Medical Center about four miles away. Upon arrival at the hospital, the doctors induced a coma in the pilot.

When Dr. Mark Griffin questioned Larry about how he was, he immediately asked the doctor, "How's the other guy?" The doctor told him that the pilot was probably not going to make it. Some time later, while Hicks was being treated for gasoline burns on his upper body, he heard the helicopters arrive to airlift the pilot to the University of Alabama Medical Center in Birmingham, where he was put on a respirator, with a trauma team working on him. After a decontamination shower, Hicks was released from the hospital.

Larry and Donna, who had been waiting for him at the hospital, headed home, but were shocked upon arriving at their gated community to find news crews waiting outside the gate for a chance to interview the police, who were still trying to get the plane out of the lake, and would not allow the media inside.

Word was out, even while the rescue was taking place, that a light plane had crashed, piloted by celebrity Jack Roush, NASCAR and Winston Cup car owner since 1988, and CEO of Roush Industries, Inc., an engineering and prototype development company in Livonia, Michigan. Earlier that day, Roush, an aircraft aficionado, had piloted his World War II vintage P-51 Mustang airplane from his Michigan home to Troy, where he was meeting friends to celebrate his 60th birthday. As a birthday present, the friends had arranged for Roush to fly the Air-Cam, a specialized aircraft built specifically for photography, and known for its use by *National Geographic*.

When Donna called the Hicks' adult son, Brian, to tell him what had happened, she told him the name of the pilot was something like Rice or Reese or Roush, but that they did not know for sure. Brian's reaction was immediate: "Jack Roush of NASCAR? Are you kidding? What planet have you been living on?"

Four hours after the accident, as he tried to relax at home, Larry said to Donna in amazement, "Did what I think happened, just happen?" He stayed up all night, unable to sleep from the after-effects of so much adrenaline pumping though his body. He watched the sunrise from his patio, finally falling asleep about 4:00 p.m. the following day.

For his part, Roush was in poor condition. He had inhaled water and gasoline and suffered closed-head injuries, rib fractures, a collapsed lung, compound fractures to his left leg, and broken ankles. He had been knocked out by a head injury when he hit the power lines, and did not remember anything from the time of the accident until he woke up in the hospital that weekend, including having gone through the drowning experience.

Six days after the accident, amazingly enough, Roush was running his business by telephone from his hospital bed. By that Sunday, he was ready for a reunion with his rescuer. He arranged for Larry and Donna to be flown by private jet to Birmingham, Alabama, where they visited him at the hospital. They walked into a room full of Jack's family and friends wearing "Roush" jackets and shirts.

By now, Larry and Donna were beginning to understand the celebrity status of Jack Roush, if for no other reason than the number of telephone calls they were receiving at their home from the news media, eager to interview Larry about his heroic rescue of the man. As Larry said later, "We must have been the only people in Alabama who didn't follow NASCAR."

When Larry and Jack looked at each other for the first time after the rescue, they hugged, and Jack said "Thank you," but they were too choked up with tears and too overcome with emotion to say more. Donna, and Jack's wife, Pauline, who was also present, started to cry. Others in the hospital room, which included Jack Jr; one of Jack's daughters and her husband, and Jack's brother, Frank, choked up, too. It seemed a good 20 minutes before everyone recovered enough to hold a normal conversation. It was then clear from what Jack said that he was humbled by his good luck in having Larry Hicks nearby when the Air-Cam went down.

Six weeks later, Roush piloted a plane from his Michigan home and hobbled around on crutches at Dover International Speedway in Dover, Delaware, overseeing his four-car Winston Cup team. Larry and Donna were by his side.

Larry Hicks has no doubt that a Higher Power was at work in Jack Roush's incredible rescue. He says he did not save him; he was just the instrument. If the Air-Cam had hit the high tension power lines instead of the support wires, the plane would have gone down in flames. If it had crashed on the ground or hit a tree in the underwater stump field where it landed, Roush undoubtedly would have been killed instantly.

If Larry and Donna had purchased the home they originally tried to buy on the other side of Palos Verdes Lake; or Larry had been late in coming home from work that day; or he and Donna had decided to go to a movie, as they had discussed, or simply been in another part of the house, they would not have seen the plane go down, and the only headline would have been that Jack Roush had died in a plane crash.

If the accident had taken place a few months earlier, Hicks, who had suffered a tremendous weight loss from the effects of chemotherapy and radiation treatment for nose and throat cancer, would not have been strong enough to pull Roush out of the water. If Wayne Hicks had not left the johnboat ready to go, the ending might have been different.

But, most amazing of all, Hicks was one of a small percentage of the populace with the specialized knowledge necessary to save a pilot in an upside-down plane from a watery grave—specialized knowledge without which there is no question but that Jack Roush would have died. And, one other thing was necessary to save Jack's life, which is that Hicks is the kind of man he is: a man of action who, even with his own less than perfect health, did not hesitate to put himself at risk to save a stranger's life.

Epilogue

Larry Hicks finds it hard to understand the recognition and accolades that have come his way as a result of his heroic rescue of Jack Roush. He says that as a Marine, he did not have the option of not doing anything. Among the many honors awarded him are the Marine Corps Medal of Heroism, the Alabama Attorney General's Law Enforcement Officer of the Year Award for the Southern District of Alabama, the Carnegie Award for Heroism from the Carnegie Foundation, the Kiwanis International Robert P. Connally Medal for Heroism, the Society of the Sons of the American Revolution Medal for Heroism, and the Alabama Legislative Law Enforcement Medal of Honor. The story of the rescue appeared in *People* magazine, twice, and Larry and Jack were on the cover of the December 2002 issue of *NASCAR Illustrated,* and other NASCAR issues in the months that followed.

Hicks and Roush have become close friends, likening their relationship to that of brothers. They both remain very emotional about the rescue. Jack says he is now "a kinder, gentler, more humorous Jack Roush," and that his greatest fear is that he won't be able to live up to the responsibility of being "given these extra days."

Larry is proud that he lived up to the United States Marine Corps Code of serving his country with "Honor, Courage, and Commitment," with selfless service. The Marine Code applies to both active duty marines and those who have retired or otherwise returned to civilian life. Larry says that other than his marriage to Donna and the birth of his children and grandchildren, this is the most special thing that has happened in his life. He is now making plans to learn to fly.

By Brenda Warneka

A Star is Watching

It was raining in Delhi that afternoon when the call came. Our telephone was out of order, so Uncle Rahman called us at the upstairs neighbor's apartment. A call at the neighbor's meant that I had to take it. My husband, Vinod, and his father were at the office, and my mother-in-law could not run up the stairs fast enough.

"Hi, Uncle!" I yelled above the din made by the pelting rain and the neighbor's washing machine, which seemed to be on the verge of breaking all sound barriers with the racket it was making.

"Hullo, Abha," he said. "I can't get through to Iyengar and Vinod at the office."

"All the lines seem to be down, Uncle," I shouted.

"Well, Abha," he said, "do you remember the writing project you and Vinod worked on for my book?"

"Yes," I answered, a sudden excitement gripping me. Our writing on "Population" was published as part of a two-volume book edited by Uncle Rahman, who previously had been Advisor on Science Policy to the Government of India and was now Director of the National Institute for Science, Technology and Development.

"The Technical University in Berlin wants one of you to present a paper on 'Urbanization and its Effect on Population' at a three-day conference there. Your air travel from India will be reimbursed, and lodging arrangements will be made for you. I will be presenting a paper, too. You and Vinod decide which one of you will go. It is in December sometime. I will give you the details later."

"I'm going," I said to him. "I will get back to you, Uncle. And thanks."

I could barely contain the excitement bubbling within me. I am a rather diffident person. I find all kinds of excuses for not doing the things I really want to do. Until then, I had immersed myself in taking care of the kids and the family. I had convinced myself that for the moment, this was all I wanted. However, one thing was definite. If anyone was going to Berlin, *I was*.

On Vinod's return from the office, I told him about Uncle's call. He was all for it. He knew that I had studied some German during my college years, and that the language and people fascinated me. I had always wanted to visit Germany. This was a Heaven-sent opportunity.

I began, in earnest, researching and writing the paper on urbanization. After submitting the draft to Uncle Rahman for evaluation, I then rewrote it and gave it the final touches. I had never presented a paper on my own, but that did not deter me. The fact that my children were just four and six years old, and I would be leaving them behind, did not daunt me. Vinod had said he would look after them and it was just a matter of a few days. Moreover, my mother-in-law was there, and I had a servant to take care of chores. The greatest opposition came from my mother-in-law. She did not like the fact that I would be leaving the children behind, or that I would be traveling alone. I had anticipated her response; usually, I succumbed to pressure, but this time, I dug my heels in.

At the same time, I was developing a touch of a cold. I went to the local doctor, and he prescribed some antibiotics. However, the medicine did not help. I was losing my appetite at the sight of food. Silly fool that I was, I was thrilled at the idea of losing weight and looking more "hip" in my jeans. I ignored what was really happening to my system and put it down to stress and last minute jitters.

My kids were also acting up (they could sense the tension around them), and my mother-in-law was still trying to dissuade me from going, telling me I was not well enough to travel. Vinod, seeing how pale I was, also tried to convince me to cancel the trip, though he knew I was hell-bent on going. I refused to budge. My Taurean temperament had come to the fore. Once he knew I would not change my mind, he supported me all the way, making things as easy for me as he could.

Hence, it came about that I flew to Berlin to attend the three-day conference. After the conference, I planned to holiday with another uncle who was going to be in England at that time and had offered to show me London for two days before I returned to India. On the second day of the conference, however, after successfully presenting my paper, I immediately became so sick that I had to be hospitalized.

It was discovered that I had Hepatitis A. The doctors believed that I had picked up the infection in India, but it had manifested itself while I was in Berlin. I was rushed to the Krankenhaus Prenzlauerberg, the largest liver treatment hospital in Berlin, where I went into a coma that same night.

I learned later that the German doctors had called Vinod and told him, "Come now, if you want to see your wife's face one last time." He flew to Germany immediately, with my father arranging for his ticket, and ten American dollars in his pocket, loaned by a relative. Vinod could not get any money exchanged because he already had gone to America earlier that year on a work-related visit, and the Indian law at that time did not allow an individual to take foreign exchange out of the country more than once a year. However, nothing on earth was going to stop Vinod from being with me.

When my distraught husband landed in Germany, a friend of my younger sister's husband was there to meet him. Jurgen did not know Vinod, but he not only came to the airport, he also offered to allow Vinod to stay at his home as long he wished. Jurgen came to the hospital the next day with chocolates and a large card, that opened up into a beautiful cutout. It showed a famous building in Berlin and a star over it, with "A star is watching over you" written in his lovely calligraphy. He had come up with this overnight, for me, a woman he was meeting for the first time. Why should a stranger do so much? Only a sense of humanity and compassion drives gentle souls like him. He is a dear friend now and forever.

It was the team of able East German doctors at the Krankenhaus (the Berlin Wall had only recently fallen) who saved my life. They did it without doing a liver transplant. They half-jokingly said that mine was an Indian liver, stronger than a European one, and so they were able to revive it. The fact was that they had to keep me alive until the papers for a liver transplant could be completed, which took longer because I was a foreigner. By the time the paperwork was done, I was already on the way to recovery, due to the doctors' relentless efforts, and I did not need the liver transplant.

How the doctors pampered me! I was their star patient. My recovery was a miracle, which even they were unable to fully comprehend. My three-day odyssey to present my paper at the conference turned into a month-and-a-half long stay in Berlin. Then, weak and frail, but bubbling with the spirit of Christmas and the New Year, which I had celebrated with new friends with whom I felt a special bond, I was ready to go home.

On my return to India, I was so weak that Vinod arranged a wheelchair for me at the airport. The sight of my family, especially the kids, made me forget everything else. As they ran forward to hug me, my eyes filled with tears. The children had been well looked after while I had been away. They now clung to me, unwilling to let go.

This separation from my family had been a necessary one, willed by the grace of God. People say that if I had stayed back, rested in India, and not taken the strenuous journey to Berlin, I would have recovered quicker. I know different. I know I was destined to go.

My reasoning is simple. Though I was not feeling quite up to par, I did not think that my condition warranted "special" attention. The local doctor had said that I had a simple "cold" and had prescribed antibiotics, which I took—a terrible thing to do to an ailing liver, I found out later! My eyes and skin did not have the yellowness that indicates jaundice. Since I did not know that I was suffering from a major illness, I would not have rested had I stayed home in India, but would have continued attending to the demands of house and family until it was too late. A relative of ours, a successful doctor, told me later that if I had been hospitalized in Delhi in my critical condition, I would not have survived. Although India has some of the world's best doctors, no hospital in India had the necessary special drugs or medical equipment to revive my liver. No liver transplant had been successfully done in India.

It was Fate that made me receive the call that rainy day; Fate that caused me to accept the offer; Fate that ensured I was where I could get specialized medical care. Fate sent me to present that paper in Berlin so that I could live. I am a firm believer in Destiny and Karma today. Jurgen said, "A star is watching over you."

Oh, yes, Jurgen, you were so right!

By Abha Iyengar

Abha Iyengar is an Indian writer who has a BA in Economics, a double diploma in Business Management, a diploma in Interior Design, and one in Multi-Media. She writes in all genres, but prefers to write creative non-fiction and poetry. She writes about women, human relationships, spirituality and design. Abha loves to travel and explore new frontiers of the world and of the mind. She contributes to several magazines and books, and hopes to publish her own motivational book one day.

Grandmother Spirits

Fate means seeing the hand of God move clearly through your life, even with your eyes closed.

—*Rusty* Fischer.

I rushed toward my front door, running late for actors' call, as the telephone rang.

"Hello." I picked up the receiver, glancing at the clock.

"Hello, this is Dr. Holmes, your dad's doctor." My breath caught in my throat.

"You asked me to call you when he reached the final stages of his illness. I saw him late this afternoon. He has perhaps a month or six weeks to live. Do you have any questions?"

The questions had already been asked a hundred times; the answers were unchanging.

"No," I responded, taking a deep breath. "No, no questions. I'll be in touch once I've thought things through. Thank you." I hung up the telephone slowly.

This was it; finally, after two and a half years of knowing what was coming. I wanted to sit down and absorb the news, to compose myself and then call my father. I looked again at the clock. No time. Our show was due to start in a little over an hour, and I should have been there already.

"The show must go on," I told myself with a new understanding of the old show business maxim. I allowed myself one quick sob, then fled to my car.

It was August 2nd, opening night of the "Days of Old Fort Hall," an outdoor historical pageant. The drama, which told of the founding of the original Idaho fort in fur-trapper days, was the culmination of months of script research, auditions, travel back and forth between town and the Fort Hall Indian Reservation, and long evenings of rehearsal with more than a hundred people. We had been working toward this night for a long time.

I was the narrator, The Storyteller, a primary role, so I had no option but to report in. As I drove, my mind was still on the telephone call and its ramifications. My feelings were hundreds of miles away with my father.

I soon arrived at the replica of the historic fort that loomed in the slanting sun like a ghost out of Idaho's past. Flanking it on either side were two tipi encampments. One encampment represented a Shoshoni village of Sacajawea's people. It teemed with sturdy brown men and women in traditional dress, shining horses, even a dog or two playing with the scampering children among the tents and campfires.

The other grouping of lodges echoed with the raucous laughter of mountain men in buckskin outfits and fur caps, knives and long-barreled black powder rifles at their sides. They jostled each other and practiced throwing tomahawks against the huge tree stump propped up at the edge of their clearing.

The villages were replicas, but both the native and the mountain man populations actually lived there for the duration of the final rehearsals and the shows. There are several organizations of mountain men who regularly hold rendezvous around the country. They live in their tipis or lodges and are very particular about everything being as authentic as possible, in dress, custom, food, lodging and activities, depicting the period, roughly, from the 1830s to the 1850s. Though full tribes don't do it anymore, there are still some Native Americans who follow the plant and animal resources to gather food, for clothing and many other uses.

Therefore, both the Shoshoni and the mountain man encampments were indeed authentic, if only for a short time. Tipis were set up, they cooked over open fires, tended to their horses and children, and of course slept there at night. Even though they were set up around a replica of the original Fort Hall, they were functional living situations. One couple even got married there!

I parked my old Volvo and went to find Joyce. Joyce was Shoshoni-Bannock, and we had become good friends after working closely together on the pageant. I found her backstage.

Joyce took my arm and steered me behind the set, among some trees. "What's wrong?"

Quickly I told Joyce of the telephone call. "Right after the final show on Saturday night, I plan to drive up to Washington to see Dad. I need to go to him!"

"Of course you do. You belong with him at the end. Does Jeff know yet?"

My son, Jeff, was somewhere in the Far East. I didn't know where exactly—either Japan or Korea. He'd talked his way aboard a cargo ship embarking from Seattle, to tour those exotic countries and to "find out a little more" about himself and his birthplace.

"No. I don't know how to get in touch with him. I have a tentative contact person in Kamakura, and will try to call her. But who knows when he'll be in touch with me? Oh, Joyce, I want so to talk to Jeff about this!"

Joyce held me close. "We'll figure something out; don't worry. You just go and get ready for this show, my sister." She gave me a gentle push toward the dressing area.

I wiped tears from my cheeks, then wandered up to where the horses were tethered. I patted the neck of a vibrant young pinto gelding whose forelock was decorated with an eagle feather. Red painted circles around his eyes and hand prints on his flanks gave him an owly, otherworldly look. I forced myself to be calm, stroking the pony, talking softly to him.

Finally, I was ready. The actors were all in their places, and as the opening music surged, I walked out on the huge outdoor stage to the microphone, awash in a bright circle of light, and began to tell the story.

Opening night excitement was high and contagious, and the show went well. Then applause rolled across the green and onto the stage as the finale soared, the lights dimmed, and it was over.

I was almost carried off my feet as the keyed-up players swarmed backstage, whooping and chattering in glee. Even the animals felt it. The horses tossed their manes as they pushed and nipped at each other and at the dogs dashing underfoot.

I worked through the melee, looking for Joyce. She found me and touched my shoulder. "Come, Emma wants to talk to you."

Emma was one of the elders, proud and wise, a deeply spiritual woman. She traveled each year to the International Peace Conference, wherever it was held, and added her prayers for universal peace to those of people from around the globe. Emma was waiting by the campfire at her tipi.

"Joyce told me about your problem. Come here; I will pray for you." The old woman held out her hand, and I took it. "Oh, Emma, I'm so worried. I need to talk to my son, and I don't know how to find him."

"Don't worry. I will pray for you to the grandmother spirits. You stand here near the fire and face the east."

The diminutive woman with weathered face and long gray hair placed one hand lightly on my shoulder. She began to pray, chanting a gentle swift song of oddly familiar words, reminding me of Japanese language rhythms I once knew. The halting melodious cadences rose on the air toward the full moon suspended in the sky. The fire beside us flickered and flared, sending sparks to follow the prayers, carrying them to their destination, as they rose higher, to be lost in the small night sounds.

Emma finished with her head held high, chin raised and eyes closed. Her lips silently formed promises of things to come. Then she sighed, opened her eyes and cast a satisfied look at me.

"Okay, it's done. You go home now and sleep. You look terrible. I'll see you tomorrow night."

I thanked Emma with a swift touch on her cheek. Joyce walked with me to my car.

We stepped carefully in our moccasins among the tipis, avoiding gear, sleeping dogs, children's games and lodge poles. I was surprised at how quiet the village had become. The prayers must have lasted longer than I realized. Families were bedding down in their lodges; fires were only embers. Soft murmurs of adult conversation drifted quietly from darkened door openings. Occasionally, a horse would stamp or snort. In the shadows under a tree, a dog yipped in dream pursuit of ghost prey.

At the Volvo, Joyce turned to me. "Emma knows what she's doing. Try to sleep tonight. She's taking care of things. I'll see you tomorrow."

The performances on Thursday and Friday nights went equally well. As I was ready to leave for the final performance on Saturday evening, the telephone rang. I hesitated, then answered.

"Hello?"

"Mom—it's Jeff!"

"Jeff! Where are you?"

"Hiroshima…"

"Hiroshima? I didn't know you were going there!"

"I wasn't. But when I got to Japan three days ago, I remembered what you said about Hiroshima and the part of the bombed-out city they kept as a Peace Park—what an impact it had on you the first time you saw it. So I decided to come here and see for myself."

I couldn't speak.

"Mom, are you still there?"

"Yes, I'm here."

"Well, I arrived in Hiroshima a little while ago, and it just happens to be the anniversary of the bomb…"

"Of course! It's August 5th here, but with the International Date Line, it's the sixth over there!"

"Yeah, and I happened to show up just at the beginning of the three hours when the city allows any foreigner to make a free three minute telephone call to anywhere in the world. So I got in line, and here I am. Isn't that great?"

"Oh, honey…you don't know how badly I needed you to call!" I started to cry.

"Mom! What's wrong?"

"Dr. Holmes called three days ago. Your grandfather has perhaps a month, maybe six weeks to live."

"Oh, wow!" I could hear the catch in his voice.

"Jeff, I wish you were here!"

"Oh, wow!" he said again, haltingly. "I need to think about this. The next guy in line wants to make his call. I promise I'll call you by Monday and let you know what I'm going to do. I gotta hang up now."

"Okay, honey. I'll wait for your call."

I replaced the receiver with a hand that trembled so badly I had to steady it with my other hand. I took a deep breath and hurried out the door.

As soon as I arrived at the village, I ran to find Emma. I found her smoke-tanning deer hides over her campsite fire.

"Emma, Emma, it's working!"

The handsome old woman looked at me intently. "Tell me. How is it working?"

In a rush of words, I related the story of my son's call, then stopped and looked at her. Emma studied me silently. She suddenly grinned.

"Of course it worked! That's the third time this month!"

Jeff traveled back to spend the last month of Dad's life with him. Dad died in our arms.

By Mary-Alice Boulter

Mary-Alice Boulter is a writer, civic activist, mother and grandmother who has traveled and lived many places in the world, but settled in Pocatello, Idaho, for the casual perspective it provides. She is proud of her father's Native American heritage. Legitimate theatre is her avocational therapy, and she has more than half a century of professional theater experience. Her family of dogs, cats, plants and books keeps her centered, and her job managing the regional office for the Idaho State Police keeps them all fed and a roof over their heads.

The Train Not Taken

Men at some time are masters of their fates: The fault...is not in the stars,
but in ourselves.

—William Shakespeare

I was a child of World War II, having been born in 1936 in Hungary. My young mother died a couple of weeks after my birth, and my father was away because of the war, so my maternal grandparents were raising me.

When you're a child of war, you're never sure what the day, next hour, or next day may bring. All you can do is hope and pray that it will all soon be over. That's what I did, day after day.

We lived in the Bacska region of Hungary, near the Serbian border, and when in 1944, Tito's communist Partisans were closing in, many Hungarians decided to leave. We were no exception. Grandfather conferred with his youngest brother, Tamas, and our two families made plans to go to Kalocsa, where Uncle Peter, my grandfather's oldest brother, lived. I was seven at the time and was happy that we'd be going together, since Uncle Tamas' youngest daughter, Kati, who was eight, was my favorite cousin.

The following couple of days were spent packing the few things we would be taking along. Most of our belongings were to be left behind. Grandmother agreed that I could take two of my favorite story books with me; the rest of my toys and books would have to be left behind.

"We can read to each other on the train," I told Kati. Reading was my favorite pastime.

"Yes, and we can watch the scenery. The train will go right by Lake Balaton," Kati said. Lake Balaton was Hungary's largest lake. We had learned about it in school, but had never seen it, so this was something we looked forward to. Kati and I also looked forward to being with our cousin, Agi, Uncle Peter's youngest child, whom we hardly knew. She was nine, and in a letter to us, she wrote that she couldn't wait to see us.

That night, before we were to leave for the train station, Grandfather suddenly had an abrupt change of plans.

"We are not taking the train. We are going in the wagon, instead," he announced.

"But it will take you ten days by wagon. By train, you'll be there in two days," said Uncle Tamas.

"I know, I know. But we can pack much more into the wagon and take it along. We have very little money left. Things are expensive. Why leave the few things we still have behind?"

"Well, we are taking the train just as we planned. So we will be seeing you in about ten or eleven days," was the last thing Uncle Tamas said before he left for home.

Of course I was upset by Grandfather's change of plans. It meant that Kati and I would not be traveling together. And it also meant that Kati would get to Agi's house long before I did. That made me feel envious of her. But, I knew that once Grandfather made up his mind about something, there would be no changing it, whether I liked it or not.

All that night, my grandparents worked on packing things into the horse-drawn wagon. (Cars were still a rarity in our part of the world back then.) Early the following morning, while the guns of the Partisans could be heard in the distant hills, we boarded the wagon and left the village of our birth, for good.

Once the wagon was on the road, and I was comfortably snuggled into my featherbed in the back of the wagon, the journey got more interesting. There were hundreds of people on the road with their wagons—all of them hoping to find safety somewhere in our country. When we heard war planes approaching, we'd all scramble out of our wagons and run and lie down in a ditch, just in case those silver cigars above us would decide to drop some bombs.

At night, we camped together, somewhere along the road, and the men built little fires so the women could cook our meager suppers. And again, if we heard war planes heading our way, people rushed to put out the fires and ran for ditches or the nearby woods, with prayers on their breath!

On the fifth day of our journey, we reached Lake Balaton. I gazed at the shimmering waters and thought of Kati. There were beautiful villas along the lake, and I wondered if the people living in them felt safer in their placid lake homes. Grandfather said he doubted it.

We found a public area of the lake and took the horses for a drink, while we washed our hands and faces for the first time in days. Then we went on, joining the posse of wagons again.

Finally, after what seemed like an eternity to a seven year old, we arrived in the city of Kalocsa, and soon pulled into Uncle Peter's property. Uncle Peter and

Aunt Roszi came running out of the house to greet us, followed by Agi and her teenage brother, Imre.

"Where are Tamas and his family?" I heard Grandfather ask, as I was getting ready to jump to the ground.

"You mean you haven't heard?" Uncle Peter asked, his expression turning grave.

"Heard what?"

"The train they were traveling on got hit by bombs. Everyone on that train was killed. Blown to bits beyond recognition. It was on the radio. I thought you knew by now."

I'll never forget my grandfather's reaction upon hearing the news that his "baby" brother was gone. He buried his face in his hands and sobbed uncontrollably. It was the first time I had seen him cry.

"I told him I had a bad feeling about taking the train. But he wouldn't listen," Grandfather kept saying over and over, while Grandmother held me close and tried her best to comfort me, for I was crying, too.

"It's my fault Kati never got here," I wailed broken-heartedly. "I was jealous of her getting here ahead of me. I wished we could get here first." I don't think I ever totally got over the guilt.

This was my first close experience with the reality of war, and it left an indelible mark on me. But there would be many more close calls before that terrible war finally ended. We were among the lucky ones. We survived, later fled our Soviet-occupied country, and after four years in a refugee camp, were allowed to immigrate to our wonderful new country, the United States.

Why were we among the lucky ones? Only God knows the answer to that question.

By Reni Burghardt

Renie S. Burghardt is a free-lance writer who was born in Hungary and came to the United States in 1951. Her works have been published in many magazines and anthologies such as, *Chicken Soup; Chocolate for Women; Cup of Comfort; Listening to the Animal*, and *God Allows U-Turns*, among others. She enjoys reading, gardening, observing nature, spending time with her granddaughters, and tending some small animals that she raises on her farm in the Ozark Mountains of Missouri.

Plato Never Swamped a Dozer

"Hey, Hack!" my track team buddy Larry yelled to me from the window of his old Ford. "You find a summer job yet?"

We'd just graduated from high school in one of the sleepy little valley towns of Appalachian Pennsylvania, class of '57. And we'd both been accepted at Penn State. But I'd be starting in the fall *only* if I had enough money for tuition, which in those days was a lot more reasonable than it is now. Still, I didn't have it. Mom and Dad said they'd cover my living expenses, but they couldn't afford tuition, too. I needed to come up with five hundred dollars.

"Nope," I confessed to Larry. "And I've looked everywhere. Dad couldn't get me in at the rayon plant because I'm not a college guy *yet.*"

Larry smiled. "Well, you're in luck then, man. My cousin Bill from Mifflintown called *his* dad last night. Up in Painted Post, New York. They need *dozens* of guys on the gas pipeline they're laying up there. Bill's bringing one of his friends. You wanna go along?"

It was like a gift from heaven. In those days, I would have said that Fate had opened a doorway for me, and all I had to do was pack my suitcase and walk through it. I talked to my parents, and they said it was all right. Mom sniffled a little; it would be my first time away from home. Dad got kind of serious. He warned me that pipeline work was dangerous sometimes. He'd worked construction for a while when he was my age.

Sure, right. I'd be careful. What's a little danger to an eighteen year old? At that age, when you think you're going to live forever—when you believe that nothing bad could ever happen to *you?*

We left late that next Sunday night, after I'd said goodbye to the girl I'd been dating. Larry's cousin Bill drove. To my surprise, Larry's friend, Jack, who also sat up front, was black. There'd been only one black student, Fenton Short, in my high school, and I'd never been in any classes with him.

We talked about what working on a pipeline would be like most of the way up there, but Jack didn't say much.

We got to the pipeline office at dawn, and they hired us on the spot—at least they hired Bill and Larry and me. They took Jack's application and told him they'd call in a day or two. We were kind of surprised. We thought that maybe we should go back home since they didn't want to hire Jack. He told us to go ahead and take the jobs. He'd find something else to do.

It didn't seem right, but that's what we did. They hauled the three of us out to the job site, a railroad siding where we unloaded 50-foot sections of pipe covered with grease. We worked in the same clothes we had ridden up in, doing back-breaking labor. Twelve hours later, we were exhausted, and covered in graphite grease from our noses to our shoes.

Jack was waiting for us with Bill's car, and he laughed when he saw us. We drove around looking for a place to stay that night, but no motel would take us because we were so dirty.

We showed up at the pipeline office just as dirty as when we'd left, but they didn't care. The woman at the desk asked us where our friend Jack was. We learned later that Bill's dad had come in and raised hell because they didn't hire Jack.

Larry ran out and caught Jack just as he was pulling out of the parking lot. I thought Jack would tell them to shove their damned job, but he didn't. The upshot was that Jack was hired, and he and I were sent over to South Mountain, while Bill and Larry stayed with the pipe-unloading job.

Jack cut brush, but they said I was going to be a swamper on a dozer. I told the foreman that I'd never worked with heavy equipment, but he said I could pick it up as I went along.

A swamper greases the "Cat," fuels it up, adjusts the angle of the blade when needed, sets or moves stakes for the driver, and a hundred other things, about most of which I was completely ignorant. It didn't take the Cat driver long to fig-ure out that I didn't know what the hell I was doing.

"He's what they sent me!" the foreman yelled when the driver complained. "Teach him!"

At the end of the day, the foreman told us about a lady who lived nearby who would rent Jack and me a room. Over the next few weeks, I got to know Jack well. His job was a lot harder than mine, but he never complained about it.

After a week, the Cat driver stopped trying to tell me what to do and just got off and did it himself. That meant I was standing around most of the day. Another guy swamping *did* show me how to gas the Cat up, grease it, and check the radiator. But that's all I really learned.

Two weeks before I was going to quit to start college, the foreman came up to me and handed me a slip of paper. "You were about ready to hang it up anyway, weren't you?"

Jack took the news harder than I did. They hadn't taught me right, he maintained. I told him it was all okay; not to worry about it. I had seven hundred dollars in my pocket, so I didn't mind having a couple of weeks off before classes started. But I did appreciate that Jack was on my side.

The next morning before he went to work, we shook hands, said goodbye, and a Greyhound bus took me home. I never saw Jack again.

Right before college started, Larry telephoned. "You'll never guess what happened to the guy who took your job." The next Monday morning, the new swamper had been killed. He'd opened the radiator cap to check the fluid level after the engine had been running, and the cap had hit him right between the eyes. Killed instantly, his head smashed in.

"You are one lucky son-of-a-bitch," Larry told me. I thought I was lucky, too, and still think so.

I've never believed in the ancient Greek's idea of Fate—that everything that happens to you is mapped out somewhere. That there's really nothing you can do about it, if like Oedipus, it's predetermined that you're going to kill your father and marry your mother.

To me, a different way of looking at Fate makes more sense: that what you *do*—your decisions—determine what happens to you later on. Of course, you never know what anything will mean later on. For example, if I'd never met and learned to like Jack, I never would have made friends with a lot of black students at the *second* university I went to, after I'd flunked out of Penn State and worked at the rayon factory for two years. And because I'd gotten to know a number of black students there, I developed an interest in African-American literature when I was working on my Ph.D., which resulted in my editing and publishing *Mandy Oxendine,* the first novel written by Charles Chesnutt, an African-American who wrote in the late 1900s. That book had been rejected by white publishers for the same reason that, at first, Jack had been turned down by the pipeliners. In a way, Chesnutt's first novel is available in libraries today because I was lucky enough to get to know a bright, funny young black guy named Jack on a construction job a long time ago. *That's* Fate.

By Charles Hackenberry

Charles Hackenberry, Ph.D., is a college professor and free-lance writer who lives in the Bald Eagle Valley of Central Pennsylvania with his wife, Barbara, and surrogate grandson, Bobby, a four-year-old terrier or terrorist, depending on the day. He teaches various writing and literature courses, and is an award winning novelist.

Freddy Lucks Out

Both my parents were natives of England. I was born in 1917 during a bombing raid by German Zeppelins while my father was serving as a pilot with the Royal Air Force in North Africa. When World War I ended, my parents decided to try their fortune, first in Toronto, Canada, and then in Detroit, Michigan.

Listening to my father's stories about the "romance of the air," I developed a love for airplanes at an early age. My youth was spent reading and dreaming about flying. I made models, both rubber band and gas powered, and spent hours flying them in the summer skies. I couldn't wait until I was old enough to get into the "flying business." I majored in aeronautical design at Cass Technical High School in Detroit and decided that when I graduated, I would try to get a job in one of the many airplane factories in the Detroit area.

However, like most displaced Englishmen, my parents wanted to go "home." Although they had a host of friends in the States, they had both left large families, whom they missed more with each passing year. After my grandmother died in England, my parents decided that they should return to live near their families. Notwithstanding that I was 19, and it meant leaving all my friends and interrupting my education, we returned to England in the mid-1930s.

My father, being an American-trained Production Engineer, soon found a position with a large company, making heavy forgings and presses. I continued my schooling in Aeronautics at the Polytechnic Institute and, for a period, at Christ Church at Oxford, before getting a degree in Aeronautics from the University of London.

I was working in Research and Development with Omes Ltd. in Barnes, and I had an arrangement with the management that when my berth came up in the fall, I would be free to join Handley Pages, a major aircraft factory, in Cricklewood. Pages was one of the finest aircraft companies in England.

After British Prime Minister Neville Chamberlain returned from Munich in 1939, and gave his "Peace in our time" speech, we knew it was just a matter of time before we would be at war with Germany. Therefore, a number of us from the Polytechnic Institute volunteered to join the Royal Air Force as technical officers. As my specialty was aircraft design, I would be assigned to Farnborough, the RAF research station, if and when war broke out. However, the RAF research group did not have facilities ready to receive the required personnel, so I was only away from home for two weeks while I attended a preliminary orientation program. This would save time if hostilities broke out, and I was called to serve.

Hitler moved into Poland, and war was declared on September 3rd, 1939. I was called into active service on the 10th, receiving my commission and being posted to the Royal Air Force research division at Farnborough, where I spent the remainder of the war.

Three of us who had been students together at the Polytechnic Institute arrived at Farnborough the same day: Reggie Bicknell, Freddy Dennet, and myself. Reggie opted to room with a senior technician he knew, leaving Freddy and me as roommates.

Freddy and I had been in a number of classes and lectures together over the years, and always finished within a place or two of each other in our final examinations, but we ran with different crowds.

Freddy's preference was anything having to do with politics, while I had attached myself to a group whose interests were the arts, photography, and traveling around the countryside. However, once we had settled in, we found we had a number of common interests and became fast friends.

With usual military efficiency, the wind tunnel group received a requisition for two technical officers with the rank of Flight Lieutenant for dispatch duty. We had heard of this "special duty." It entailed the officer reporting to an air base, where he received a top-secret envelope, and was promptly put on an airplane to be transported to a prearranged destination. After he delivered the envelope, he rested, if necessary, and then returned home.

I had heard stories of carriers who had been sent to parts of the States or Canada and had spent this "rest time" enjoying freedom from the war with excellent food and accommodations.

Freddy and I were selected for this special duty. We both had the same education, time in the shops, and experience in and around aircraft. Our assignments were placed in a hat, and we drew for the proposed journeys.

I drew Australia, and Freddy got the Americas. I tried to reason with him that, as neither of us had ever been to Australia, it didn't make any difference which of us went "down under." But, as I had grown up in Michigan, and I knew Americans, I was sure that once I arrived in America and explained the situation to them, they would somehow manage to snafu my visit enough to allow me to get to Detroit, and see my friends. Finally, after I promised him some of my ration points, Freddy agreed. We switched assignments, packed for a few days, and reported to the designated airfield.

That afternoon, I took off with other RAF officers and Royal Navy personnel in a Wellington Bomber. I knew from its profile, it was equipped with extra fuel tanks, and that since it was only lightly armed, we were not flying into a war zone. Our destination had to be the East coast of the United States.

By watching the stars, we knew we were flying West. After a few hours, we landed somewhere for fuel; we guessed Iceland. Then, after many more hours in the air, we landed again. This time we were allowed to de-plane to stretch our legs. While the plane was being refueled, we were brought hot food and beverages, but we were kept isolated from the hangers and the barracks.

Once we were airborne again, heading South, we began speculating as to our final destination: New York, Florida, a Caribbean Island, or a rumored research laboratory in Brazil. We finally fell asleep, and it was dark when the airship touched down onto a concrete strip. We gathered our gear and left the plane.

There were a number of Jeeps with American GIs waiting for us. An officer called my name, and I climbed into one of the vehicles. As we drove, I tried to find out where we were, but the driver kept the conversation to mundane subjects. We arrived at a small building that had sentries at the door. They presented arms (they didn't have to, as my rank did not rate it), and I was ushered into the Commanding Officer's quarters. I pulled up into a salute, and gave him the envelope. I felt rather glad we didn't have to give passwords and counter passwords, as I was sure I would have felt like a bloody fool. He returned my salute, and, as he took the envelope, said, "Lieutenant, there is a canteen down the hall where you can get some food and a rest while waiting for your return flight."

"Return flight?" I cried. "I don't even know where I am—to return from."

The Colonel smiled. "As you are not going on anywhere, it doesn't make any difference where you are, does it?"

I had something to eat, and although I tried my best, it was impossible to ascertain whether the airfield was located in the States, or if it was even in North America. The personnel, some of whom were pilots, questioned me about the war over England and in Europe. I told them what they wanted to know about the existing aircraft and losses, both the RAF and the American 8th Air Force. I was hoping they would trade information with me. But, before they could say anything, my name was called, and I was winging it back, I assumed, to England, with dreams of spending some time in Detroit rapidly fading with each drone of the engines.

On the other hand, Freddy did not return immediately from Australia, and it was weeks before we heard the reason. The Air Ministry had decided that an aircraft plant was to be built in Australia, to assemble and build certain types of light aircraft that were required in their theater of the war. This program was intended to ease up the difficulty of flying aircraft from either the States or England. The RAF insisted that a technical officer be in charge of the operation. When the search was made for this officer, it was found that Freddy was the only trained technical officer in the country.

Therefore, Wing Commander Freddy Dennet was now put in charge of this new operation.

Freddy held that position (with a raise in rank) until the fall of Japan, and the end of the war. However, after the halt of hostilities, the Australian government did not want to lose this new aircraft industry with the many jobs it provided, so they managed to have the operation sold to a newly-formed private company.

It was an obvious move at this point to ask Freddy, who had managed the plant all during the war, to assume the position of Director of the project.

Freddy's rank during the war, coupled with the influence he had, due to his position in the factory, allowed him to meet all the families of the "social set" in Western Australia. The first year after the war, he married the daughter of a family that owned a department store, something like Selfridges on Oxford Street in London. Working together, Freddy and his new father-in-law acquired many small businesses, both retail clothing and small engineering works, all of which were successful—making Freddy a very rich man.

After the war, when I had decided to return to America, I was clearing out some old papers and found Freddy's wedding invitation. I had to laugh at this turn of events, and could not resist writing to him. I had not seen him since we had traded assignments, and he had ended up in Australia at my behest.

He was happy to hear from me, and reminded me that his success in Australia was due to me insisting that we trade assignments that day that seemed so long ago. He offered to pay my expenses to move to Sydney and assured me of a well-paying position in one of his establishments. I declined his most generous offer, telling him I had accepted a position with an aircraft factory in California.

By Reggie Maxwell

Reggie Maxwell retired in 1987 from an engineering company in Detroit, Michigan, where he was Vice President of Research. His lifetime interest in flying waned, and he now spends his time pursuing his interest in photography and writing short stories and novels for the reading pleasure of family and friends.

"Freddy Lucks Out" is an adaptation from his (unpublished) book *Mitch*. He lives in Huntington Woods, Michigan, with his wife Marva.

Tara's Journey

Fate is a power beyond my control that determines what happens. Can I change it? Yes and no. By studying the consequences of the situation, I can sometimes soften the results.

—*Garnet Hunt White*

I wonder about one of life's great mysteries: why an inevitable safety net catches some young people and lets others fall through.

My daughter Tara began using marijuana when she was about fifteen. Her personality changed from kind, loving, and considerate to distrustful and belligerent. She stopped being an excellent student who was active in gymnastics, basketball, and martial arts, and started hanging out with friends at late night parties. I thought this was typical teenage rebellion at first. Then I discovered a marijuana pipe that she carelessly left lying around her bedroom.

When I confronted her, she denied any drug use and said the pipe belonged to a friend. For over a year, her behavior continued to deteriorate, and there were many outbursts between us. I even arranged a meeting with a family therapist, hoping to find some solutions that would make our home life more tolerable, but the counselor couldn't get Tara to admit that she was a marijuana user.

Tara's habit escalated to the point that she skipped school, drove with other students to remote locations, and spent her days getting high. Desperate to resolve the situation, I finally decided to have her tested for drugs. The day before her appointment, Tara packed up her belongings and moved out of the house. She went to live with her father from whom I had been divorced for many years. Even though my ex-husband lived in the same town, we had no communication, and he had no idea what was happening with Tara. I knew he would refuse to speak to me on the phone or in person, so I wrote him a letter.

It was useless; he did not believe me. However, it wasn't long before Tara's father discovered she had a problem. Things between them soon escalated out of control. So much so, that he didn't object when she drifted toward living with

75

her best friend, Jennifer. Jennifer's mother gave the girls the freedom they wanted.

Jennifer's family lived near my home. When I learned that Tara had taken up residence there, I immediately filed a referral with the Sheriff's Office. After I told Tara what I had done, she moved back to her father's house. Things between them did not improve, so she called and asked to come back home.

A month later, Tara and I attended a hearing in Juvenile Court, presided over by Judge Mullins, who, in a very calm and direct manner, told Tara the consequences if she continued down her chosen path. He pointed out there was evidence that she was using marijuana, and combined with falling grades, this did not bode well for her.

The judge told Tara that because she refused to listen to her parents, she had to answer to society. Her curfew was set for 8:00 p.m. on week nights and 11:00 p.m. on weekends. She was to check in with the Probation Office at appointed times and be tested periodically for drugs. In addition, she had to attend weekly drug and alcohol abuse meetings. She was to go to school every day and attend all classes. If she strayed from these conditions, there would be another hearing, the rules would become more stringent, and she could be sent to a juvenile home. In such places, the judge said, there would be no freedom. She would be told when to get up, when to eat, when to watch TV, and when she could make a phone call. In essence, her freedom would be taken away.

I will always be grateful to Judge Mullins for attempting to make Tara realize the seriousness of the situation. Tara and I both left the small courtroom in tears.

The judge did not realize it, but by restricting Tara's activities, he may have saved her life. Less than a week after the hearing, Jennifer made plans to visit relatives living about two hundred miles away. Jennifer's cousin, Denise, who had been visiting from out of town, and was returning home, pleaded with Jennifer and Tara to go back with her for a few days. Jennifer had already made up her mind to go, and told Tara they would have a great time partying with Denise.

But it was too soon. Tara had not had a chance to prove she could behave herself, and she knew she would never receive permission to go; not from the judge or me. Downhearted, she said goodbye to her friends.

The next day, Jennifer and Denise left, but they never made it to Denise's house. They were close to the end of their trip when Jennifer asked Denise to let her drive. They had been drinking throughout the journey, and even though Jennifer had very little experience behind the wheel, she wanted to drive. Denise was easily convinced. Soon afterwards, Jennifer misjudged a curve in the road and lost control of the car. She was thrown through the windshield because she didn't have her seatbelt on and was killed outright. Denise, who had been wearing her seatbelt, suffered a broken arm.

Tara did not get the news directly; it came to her by way of a friend. She called me at work, hysterical. It was impossible for her to believe that Jennifer was dead. Hadn't she just spoken to her the previous day? *How could it be?* The shock of losing her friend under such tragic circumstances was very difficult for Tara's teenage mind to comprehend. Death did not come to healthy, young girls.

Several days later, Jennifer was brought back home so that family and friends could say goodbye. Her cousin Denise, with her arm in a cast and sling, was a stark reminder of the accident that ended Jennifer's short life.

Jennifer had chosen to be an organ donor and had been on life support after the accident so that her vital organs could be used to save other lives. Her mother had acquiesced to Jennifer's decision. I was amazed that someone so young would think ahead to make such a decision.

At Jennifer's memorial service, Tara and others spoke about what Jennifer meant to them. Tara wrote a long poem, but the part that touched me most was when she said: "They say that hearts don't really break, but that's not true. For today, when Jennifer is laid to rest, it breaks our hearts in two."

Tara has a written reminder of her friend that she keeps in her scrapbook. In a poem entitled "The Trizick and the Snow Cricket," Jennifer wrote: "The trizick and the snow cricket will rule forever, because the friendship we have will never die. She will always be in my heart, for the trizick and snow cricket will never part."

Jennifer had loved dolphins and the ocean. A few days after the memorial service, her mother took her ashes to the sea to spread on the waves. She invited Tara along, but Tara was already back in school and couldn't take a week off, which is how long Jennifer's mother was gone. On the morning that Jennifer's mother spread the ashes, dolphins appeared and played very close to shore.

Many things plague my mind about Jennifer's death. Mostly, I think about the circumstances that prevented Tara from being with her best friend on that fatal trip. For someone as young as Jennifer to have become an organ donor is enough to make me question whether she had a subconscious premonition that her life would be short-lived.

Jennifer's death had a profound effect on Tara and her friends. They all had had their drivers' licenses for some time, but before Jennifer's death, they rarely strapped on their seatbelts, even when under the influence of alcohol or drugs. And, most of them had already been involved in minor fender-benders. Since Jennifer's death, the drug use has stopped, they no longer drink and drive, and they make it a point to always fasten their seatbelts. Perhaps Jennifer's death saved other lives.

One thing is sure: her tragic death will never be forgotten by Tara who could just as easily have accompanied her down that ill-fated road.

By Patricia Hopper Patteson.

Patricia Hopper Patteson is a native of Dublin, Ireland, now residing in West Virginia. She has a BA and Certificate in Creative Writing from West Virginia University, where she received honors, including the "Waitman Barbe Creative Writing Award," and the "Virginia Butts-Sturm Award." Between 1996 and 2002, she received ten awards from the annual West Virginia Writers' Contest in non-fiction, fiction, and novel categories. Patricia has been published in *Appalachian Heritage, Blue Ridge Country, The Good Life, The Romantic, Woman's Way* (Ireland), and the anthology, *Mist On The Moon*.

Twister of Fate

Sometimes an hour of Fate's serenest weather strikes through our changeful sky in its coming beams.

—Bayard Taylor

I had only six weeks to hire a highly-specialized employee for the multi-million dollar project I was running for a large software company in Silicon Valley. I needed someone who was conversant in an arcane type of computer language used most frequently for technical documentation. If I didn't find this employee in six weeks, I would lose the requisition to hire someone. If I didn't hire an employee at all, the project was at high risk of failure, and my career could be over.

Because the extremely small number of people who knew this language worked for the government or government contractors, I frenetically started recruiting these sources nationwide. After interviewing one dud after another, I finally found a great candidate. She and I talked at length on the phone about her credentials and the job, and we were both excited. I wangled permission to fly her out from Oklahoma for a personal interview, something my company rarely allowed.

When Barbara and I met in person, we immediately hit it off. She knew the material cold, was intelligent, and funny. With blood-red fingernails, jet-black hair and punk jewelry, she was not at all what I had expected from Oklahoma. She was perfect in every way for the job, and I told her so. However, since the job would necessitate a move, she would need to discuss it with her boyfriend. We agreed to talk again the middle of the following week.

Barbara called me as promised, but not with the news I had anticipated. She had talked to her boss candidly about her new job prospects, and her boss had offered her a huge raise and a management position in response, something she never had anticipated. It was the job she had always wanted, her dream job, and she had, of course, accepted it. She wished me luck with my search. I was devastated.

The time flew by, and I was about to run up against my deadline. With only two days left to hire someone, there was no one even interesting enough to interview. I had used every recruiting tool I could think of—contacted every organization, attended tradeshows and job fairs, talked to recruiters, and checked Webster's, a job placement service on the Internet. I was out of options.

Then I thought of Barbara! Maybe she didn't like her new job, but didn't feel comfortable enough to call and tell me! It seemed highly unlikely after two short weeks, but I thought I could cover up my brazenness by saying I was calling to see if she knew someone whom she could recommend for the job. I made the call, and asked her how things were going—how she liked her new job in management.

"I hate it!" she told me, flat out.

"Enough to leave?" I asked.

Without a second of hesitation, she responded, "When can I come out?"

She and her boyfriend moved to California one week later. She loved the job, loved the environment, and was thrilled that she and her beau had made the move. She was a dedicated worker, and wowed everyone with her knowledge and savvy. It was a perfect match, and we were both very happy.

We joked about how fortunate it was for both of us that I had dared to call her back on a whim.

One day about two months after she started working with us, I was surprised to see her waiting by my office door when I arrived at work. I was an early bird, and she usually arrived much later. She looked shaken, and her red eyes made it clear that she had been crying.

"Thank you for saving my life," she said.

Confused, I joked, "Why, was the job that bad?"

"No, you don't understand. I just talked to a friend who lived down the street from me. A twister hit my old neighborhood early this morning, and leveled our old apartment building in Oklahoma. Everyone was killed."

We were both very thankful that I had acted on my impulse to call her two months earlier.

By Jan Tyler

Jan Johnson-Tyler lives in the San Francisco Bay Area and holds a BA from the University of California at Berkeley in English Literature. She is a Smithsonian Laureate for her work in electronic publishing, a writer, wildlife rehabilitator, social and community activist, and most importantly, a wife and mother. She is enjoying an early retirement and hopes to publish her first novel before going completely gray.

The Amazing Tablecloth

Many families were separated by the Nazis during World War II, never to see each other again—at least not in this life. There were some Survivors, however, who were fortunate enough to re-connect after the war; albeit, in some cases, not until many years later. How did these people find each other? Some through government agencies; others through networking or word of mouth, and still others, in more recent years, through the Internet. But, there were also those who found each other, perhaps after giving up the likelihood or possibility (but never the hope), through "the touch of fate." Following is one such story, told by Rabbi Adam Glickman, of the AG Beth Israel Synagogue, in Chicago, Illinois, during a Rosh Hashanah (Jewish High Holy Day) service.

A rabbi and his wife relocated to a new synagogue. The couple arrived in early July excited about their opportunities in this previously unknown community. The synagogue was run-down and needed a lot of work. Their goal was to be ready for Rosh Hashanah, one of the holiest of the Jewish holidays, which takes place in autumn. They worked very hard, repairing the Holy Ark, plastering the walls and painting the synagogue. They finished mid-August, ahead of schedule.

Only a few days before Rosh Hashanah, a terrible driving rain hit the area, lasting two days. Immediately after the storm, the rabbi returned to his synagogue. His heart sank when he saw that the roof had leaked, causing a large area of plaster, about 6 by 8 feet, to fall off the front wall of the sanctuary.

While cleaning up the mess, the rabbi asked God for a miracle. On his way home, he noticed a local business having a flea market sale for charity, so he stopped in. One of the items was a beautifully hand-crocheted tablecloth. It had fine colors and the Star of David (an ancient Jewish symbol) embroidered right in the center. It was just the right size to cover up the hole on the front wall.

Rushing back to the synagogue, he saw an older woman running to catch a bus, which she missed. The rabbi invited her inside to wait for the next bus. She sat in the sanctuary and paid little attention to the rabbi while he got on a ladder to hang the tablecloth as a wall tapestry. It looked beautiful. Then he noticed the woman walking down the aisle. Her face was white as a sheet. "Rabbi," she asked, "where did you get that tablecloth?"

Before he had a chance to reply, she asked him to please check the lower right corner to see if the initials "EBG" were crocheted into it. They were.

These were the initials of the woman, and she had made this tablecloth 35 years before, in Austria. The woman could hardly believe it as the rabbi told how he had just obtained the tablecloth. The woman explained that before the war, she and her husband were a well-to-do family. When the Nazis came, she was forced to leave. Her husband was going to follow the next week. She was captured, sent to a concentration camp, and never saw her husband or her home again.

The rabbi wanted to give her the tablecloth, but she told him to keep it for the synagogue. He insisted on driving her home, feeling that it was the least he could do. She lived on the other side of town and was only in the area for the day. Upon reaching her home, he graciously thanked her.

The following day, the Rosh Hashanah service was beautiful. The synagogue was almost full and the prayer sounds were like music. At the end of the service, everyone said to each other, "May you be written and inscribed in the Book of Life for a good year." One older man, whom the rabbi recognized from the neighborhood, continued to sit and stare at the wall. The rabbi wondered why he wasn't leaving. The man asked him where he had gotten the tablecloth on the wall because it was identical to the one his wife had made years ago when they lived in Austria. His wife's initials were "EBG."

The rabbi asked if the man would go for a ride with him. When he asked why, the rabbi just said to trust him; he would find out in good time. The man agreed and they drove to a house on the other side of town. The rabbi helped the man to the door and knocked. When the woman opened the door, the rabbi witnessed the most incredible reunion and biggest miracle he had ever seen.

As told by Rabbi Adam Glickman

Mabel's Dream

This is a case of not being in the wrong place at the wrong time. The year was 1959. Mabel and I were both teachers at Castaic Elementary School in Castaic, California. I lived 30 miles south of the school in Burbank, so I took my three sons to the school in Castaic. Mabel lived even further away in Glendale.

After Mabel had major surgery, she asked to meet me part way each morning so she didn't have to drive all the way to work. We began meeting at seven o'clock in the corner of a small strip-mall parking lot and leaving her car there. Early one morning, before I left my house, Mabel phoned.

"I feel bad about taking up space in that parking lot all day," she said. "Will you meet me around the next corner? I'll leave my car on the residential street."

"Okay by me," I agreed.

As Mabel was getting into my car at seven that morning, we heard an enormous CRASH! Driving back by the parking lot, we saw a small, private plane, a Funk. It had crashed, upside down, in the corner where we would have been at that very moment had Mabel parked her car there that morning.

"How did you know, Mabel?" I asked.

"I dreamed it last night," she replied. "But I didn't want to tell you it was a dream. I thought you might think I was silly to pay attention to a dream. And, I didn't know if it would really happen."

"Thank God, you acted on it," I said.

"Wow!" said my son Brad from the back seat, which was exactly how I felt.

Mabel's dream experience launched me on a lifetime of self-directed and academic study of dreaming. Later, I taught "Dream Study" at a community college and authored books telling what I learned about dreams. Today I am considered an expert on dreams.

By Janice Baylis

Janice Hinshaw Baylis, Ph.D., was born in Beloit, Wisconsin, in 1928. She moved with her parents to Burbank, California, in 1944. In 1950 she graduated from Occidental College with a BA in Education. She taught elementary school until her retirement in 1986. In 1979 she earned her MA in Psychology from Pepperdine University; 1981 saw a Doctorate in Psychology from Columbia-Pacific University. The mother of three sons and grandmother of five, Dr. Baylis is the author of *Sleep On It! The Practical Side of Dreaming*, and *Sex, Symbols and Dreams*.

Fate Springs Maternity

The heart is its own fate

—*Phillip James Bailey*

As a young woman, accustomed to getting what I wanted in life, I didn't think prayer or divine intervention would enter into my life cycle. I theorized that the only fate I was not in control of was my own birth and death and that everything in between these two events was forged by either my parents or myself. I believed God gave us the ability to make our own decisions and that fate was not preordained, predetermined, or divine destiny. With the adoption of my youngest daughter twenty-three years ago, however, my understanding of fate changed. Fate *is* real, and I have no doubt that fate is as simple as God's Will.

I married young, at nineteen. By twenty-one, I was happily pregnant. In my seventh month, I experienced the onset of early labor, and my oldest daughter was born, weighing in at four pounds, 1-1/2 ounces, but otherwise healthy. Ecstatic about being a mother, I wanted another baby right away. After three years and still no baby, I began to consider the fact that maybe I had no control over what I wanted most. I started to do something I had never done. I started to pray. I prayed constantly, morning, noon and night. I prayed for another baby. I prayed to anyone I thought would listen. Some Christians pray to Saints, some to Jesus, others pray to the Virgin Mary. I hit them all, afraid to leave anyone out. And I prayed to God, thinking He had the final say.

He answered, or at least I thought He did. I was pregnant again. I still felt in control of my own fate because, with God's help, I was getting what I wanted. Or was I? My pregnancy ended in miscarriage after twenty-two weeks. Less than a year later, another pregnancy, a boy, also miscarried at twenty-four weeks. I was torn between feeling betrayed and feeling very fortunate that I had been blessed with one beautiful daughter. I comforted myself with her presence and tried to accept that I might never have the big family I had always wanted. However, it wasn't long until I realized I was pregnant for a fourth time. Renewed with hope,

I once again prayed for a healthy child. Could this time be the answer to my prayers?

I was three months into the pregnancy; it was late summer, and I was feeling good. I decided to visit my parents in northern Minnesota. While there, my younger sister suggested that she and I go to the beach. I am not, nor have I ever been, a beach person, and being pregnant, I really didn't want to go. It was an uncharacteristic thing for me to do. I finally agreed because my daughter thought it was a wonderful idea, and my sister was so adamant about it.

It was there, on the beach with my sister, that I met a woman who at the time was six months pregnant. Knowing her casually, my sister started talking to her. The woman confided how unhappy she was about her pregnancy. Her husband had left her and her first child when she told him she was pregnant again. She believed if she were not pregnant, he would come back to her. A strange kinship developed. I wished her well, and as a gesture of good will before we left, I gave her my phone number in Minneapolis, telling her to call me if she were ever in town.

My labor started early. I wasn't yet seven months pregnant when my baby girl was born, weighing a little over one pound. I remember thinking of a pound of butter. So tiny. I named her Jolene Marie. Her condition was critical, but I thought my prayers had been answered. On her second day of life, her condition started to deteriorate. By the third day, she was having small strokes and seizures.

The doctor wanted a decision as to whether to continue the life support system. By then, he was reasonably sure Jolene was blind, possibly deaf, and the small strokes she was having could be producing retardation. "She is dying," the doctor told us. "If you are waiting for a miracle, a miracle will happen whether we shut off the life support or not." I held her for the first and last time. She died in my arms.

I gave up. As I stood at Jolene's grave, I came to the realization that I had had enough warnings. I did not want to bury another baby, and I did not want to knowingly bring a child into this world with massive disabilities. I felt betrayed. I stopped praying.

Three months, almost to the day, I received a phone call. It was from the woman I had met on the beach that previous summer. She had found a beach bag in her car trunk. In the bag was my phone number. She told me she had delivered a baby girl in December. I told her I had lost mine in March. She was alone, destitute, and unable to care for her two children. She remembered our conversation on the beach and how much I wanted children. She asked me to adopt her baby.

My husband and I left immediately, not knowing if she was serious. When we found her home, it was frightening. She was living in a small, run-down deserted cabin in northern Minnesota. I found her sitting at a kitchen table with three men who were playing cards and smoking drugs. She motioned to a room off the kitchen where I could find the baby.

The first time I saw my daughter she was lying on an old stained mattress on the floor of this cabin. The window was open without screens. Flies were everywhere. She was five-and-a half-months old. Fully awake, she broke into a large smile when she saw me. Being half-Caucasian and half-Native American, she had a full head of dark hair that stuck straight up. She was a beautiful baby, and she put her arms out to me. When I picked her up, she was wet from the neck down and felt feverish. She was having difficulty breathing and seemed congested. I asked the woman if the baby was sick. She told me she had a little cold. I expressed concern because her lips were bluish. I offered to take her to the doctor. The woman said I could do what I wanted; she was my baby.

We took her to a small clinic in Deer River, Minnesota, where the doctor suggested taking her to Minneapolis for the best treatment available. She had an advanced case of pneumonia and the doctor felt she should be hospitalized. Since we lived in Minneapolis, it was our best option. We hurried the three-hour trip to the Twin Cities and admitted her to Children's Hospital where she was treated and released to us a few days later. We were told that if she had not been seen when she was, she might have died.

We named her Jennifer Lea, not knowing if she would be ours to keep. We hired a lawyer. Her natural parents went through counseling, never swaying from their decision to let us have her. No relatives came forward to take her. After six months, right after Jenny's first birthday and two days after Christmas, she became ours. Many people had a lot of negative things to say about her birth mother: How could she be so cold as to give up her child of six months? I knew different.

The first time Jenny asked about her birth mother, I gave her a picture the woman had given me. I told her how much her mother had loved her and how she wanted the best for her. Jenny always wondered why her birth mother kept her sister, and not her. The woman didn't explain anything to me; she didn't have to. I knew she was only thinking of her baby. She had run out of options. I have a lot of respect for her to this day.

When Jenny was 19, the woman called again. She wanted to see Jenny. The decision to meet her was totally Jenny's. After several days of considering it, Jenny met her birth mother and her full-blooded sister. They met a couple of times, but when they pushed Jenny about holidays and weekend visits, it was Jenny who quietly told them, "I'm glad I got to meet you. I want to stay in touch and know about all the big events in your lives. I want to be a part of your lives, but I have a family. I only need one." She hasn't, to my knowledge, heard from them again.

I can't say I was able to give Jenny a childhood free from adversity. We had our problems. She has a personality that can be challenging at times and is very headstrong, but I've always felt lucky to have her as my daughter. She is currently very happy and planning her wedding. I am very proud of her.

Was it Fate? I think so. Why was I on the beach that day? Why did I give this woman my phone number? What made her find it after so many months? Why did she call me so soon after Jolene's death and so close to Jenny's threatening death from pneumonia? Fate prepared me to be there for Jenny. God's Will ordained it to happen.

By Wendy Meckel

Wendy Meckel and her husband, Steve, live in a suburb of Minneapolis, very near both their daughters and three grandsons. Her passion, besides her family, is writing about the human drama present in all of us. Her stories are not typically biographical, but the reality of personal experience is woven within. She attempts to enrich her life from the inspiration of ordinary characters with extraordinary circumstances, as is very evident in her novel, *Red River Rising*.

The Angel That Couldn't Fly

Fate touches us all. We cannot turn a blind eye to the connections of the cosmos.

The greatest mystery of the universe no longer remains a mystery. Why did the chicken cross the road?

There were five of us in the rusty passenger van that day. We had looked forward all summer to our vacation at the end of August—an extended weekend camping trip at Virginia's Shenandoah National Park before our respective universities called my friends and me back to the classroom.

We wanted to get on the road as early as possible that Thursday afternoon to savor every bit of Shenandoah sun that we could. My original plan of action was to clock out of work at 3:00 p.m., pick up Dave, Skooter, Ed, and Eileen by 3:30, do some quick grocery shopping, and be cruising north on I-64 by four o'clock.

The drive from our hometown of Richmond to Shenandoah doesn't take much more than two hours, which would leave us with plenty of time to set up camp before the sun called it a day.

Just after 2:00 that Thursday afternoon, however, an hour shy of my quitting time, the feeder on our main printing press went out. If the project we were working on hadn't needed to be finished that day, I would have been more than happy to begin the weekend an hour early. Deadlines are deadlines, though, and as pressman for the day, I had to wait around for some techs to get the press back up and running. By 3:30, the press was feeding properly, and I was able to get back to work. I finished the job almost two hours late.

Leaving work at about 4:30, I hit the beginning of rush hour, which further delayed picking up my by then irritated friends. It wasn't until after 5:30 that we pulled out of Bill's Grub & Gear and were chugging north on I-64 in my '91 Ford van. On the radio, Kenny Rogers sang, "You got to know when to hold'em, know when to fold'em, know when to walk away, know when to run…" Our vacation had begun.

After an hour and a half of driving, heading northeast on Route 33, we all felt close to our destination. We didn't need the sign, "Shenandoah National

Park—16 miles," to know we were almost there. We could feel it. Tree tops thickened, blocking out what little sunlight remained in the sky. The road shoulder narrowed, disappearing as we began to ascend the Blue Ridge Mountains. With the ascent, my van began to show its age, but did its best to navigate the winding road at a top speed of 35 mph. Finally, we were aware of the last sign that civilization was behind us: the radio succumbed completely to static. Just as it did—just as I began to turn off the power button—Eileen screamed, "STOP!"

Without knowing the reason for Eileen's scream, I instinctively pounded the brake pedal to the floor and throttled the steering wheel with a vise-like grip. After a few feet of screeching tires, the van came to a halt. The five of us also stopped short, following the lurching lead of centripetal force.

My heart was pounding, and adrenaline coursed through my body. Chills ran down my spine. It took a moment for me to come to my senses and discover what Eileen had seen that I hadn't. A chicken.

Yes, a chicken.

And, yes, it was crossing the road.

We all stared at it in absolute amazement as the chicken, less than five yards in front of us, walked toward the other side! It was steadfast in its resolve to accomplish this simple task and gave no indication that it realized how close it had come to becoming a messy fixture on my van's front grill. Static came from the radio as I gazed at the chicken, wondering what in the heck a chicken was doing some 3,000 feet in the sky. In the Blue Ridge Mountains, no less.

As I continued to stare at the chicken, a light began to glow from around a curve in the road 20 yards ahead of us. I soon realized it was the headlights of a logging truck speeding around the bend.

It was in our lane!

I laid on my horn. There was nothing else to do; the time to react was gone. My heart seemed to stop beating. I realized with horror that the trucker's time to react was also gone. He would hit us dead on, crush the van and kill us all on impact. Then, the logging truck would send us through the guardrail and down the embankment, where we would be buried at the bottom of the mountain.

At the last possible moment, the logging truck swerved across the double white lines and back into its own lane. The entire van shook as the logging truck barreled past us at such a speed that I was certain that its brakes must have given out.

After the truck passed, it took a moment for me to realize that we were still alive. All of us remained in shocked silence, the only sound being the static from the radio. Had that chicken not crossed the road at that very moment, I certainly would not be writing this. Instead, the van would have continued on its journey and met the grill of an oncoming semi just as we turned the bend. The chicken saved us the ghastly fate of becoming road kill.

Questions entered my mind and refused to leave. They still do. Why was the logging truck speeding down the mountain in the wrong lane? What was a logging truck doing on Route 33 anyway? Taking the scenic route out of Shenandoah National Park? Did the driver miss the sign that directed, "DOWNGRADE NEXT 6 MILES: USE LOW GEAR"? What would have happened if the driver hadn't steered his rig back into the right lane? What if I hadn't stopped for the chicken?

I got out of the van. I could barely stand. With shaking legs, I placed my left hand on the van to keep my balance. It didn't work. I fell down to my knees on the asphalt road. At first, I didn't believe my eyes. It couldn't be!

But it was. Lying next to me in the middle of the road was a feather—one single white chicken feather. Suddenly, it all made sense to me. Why did the chicken cross the road? I now knew the answer to that timeless mystery. So did Eileen. And Dave. And Scooter. Even Ed, who somehow managed to sleep through the entire miracle. We should know the answer. After all, we witnessed it. Why did the chicken cross the road?

To save us.

I don't remember much about the rest of our vacation. That's just as well. The drive there was the important part.

Yes, angels do have wings. Some of them just come in different forms.

By Michael T. Dolan

Michael T. Dolan is a free-lance writer and a public relations and communications specialist living in West Chester, Pennsylvania. He is also a correspondent for the *Daily Local News*. Dolan can often be found taking long walks in wooded areas and deserted beaches, finding that trees and conch shells are often the world's best listeners.

The Sapphire Ring

When I look back over my long life, if there is one thing that leaps out at me,
it is the role of luck and chance in our lives. From this particular string of
accidental happenings all the rest followed.

—Katharine Graham

It was the early fall of 1938. I was living with my older brother, Walter, and his
wife, Blanche, in Canton, North Carolina. My parents died when I was very
young, and I had lived most of my life with Grandma in Staffordtown, a section
of Copperhill, Tennessee, but she had agreed that I could live with Walter and
Blanche while finishing high school. Grandma was 82, too old to be raising a
teenager.

I was in my junior year of high school, about to turn 16 in November, and I
was like all the other teenage girls I knew. We went to church three times on Sunday—morning church, Sunday School, and evening church—where our main
interest was boys. They flirted, by winking and smiling at us, when we were supposed to be listening to the minister or engrossed in Bible studies. It was different
then than it is now: I was very sheltered, and flirting was not expected to lead to
anything more than holding hands.

At some point, Blanche's nephew, Beryl Hall, started walking me home from
church on Sunday evenings. He then surprised me with a sapphire ring, which
Blanche decided was an engagement ring when she spotted it on my finger. She
became very upset because Beryl was 24 years old, and she thought he was much
too old for me, and that I was too young to get engaged anyway. I tried to tell her
that it was only a friendship ring. She wouldn't listen to me. She telephoned my
older sister Bonnie in Tennessee, and said I was about to marry a 24-year-old
man. I had no intention of marrying Beryl, even if he had asked me, which he
hadn't, but Blanche got Bonnie upset, too. Bonnie was 14 years older than I was,
and very protective. She wasn't about to have me marry a 24-year-old, so she
rushed down to Canton from her home in Turtletown, packed me up, and took
me back with her. I didn't have a chance to even say goodbye to Beryl.

I did not want to go back to Tennessee with Bonnie. Turtletown was in a rural area north of Atlanta, Georgia, and I did not want to live out in the country. I loved Canton. I cried bitterly when Blanche insisted that I leave with Bonnie, and I vowed to return as soon as I could. I even left my favorite dress at the home of a woman I babysat for, telling her I would be back for it. I wished with all my heart that I had never accepted the sapphire ring.

In Tennessee, my life turned out to be much like it had been in North Carolina. We still went to church three times on Sunday, and the boys flirted with the girls. I was the new girl in town, and all the boys told me how pretty I was. I could have my pick of them, with one exception. The handsomest one of all, 20-year-old JD Kimsey, who was 6'2", with a muscular build, black curly hair and deep brown eyes, pretended to ignore me. However, I could tell he was interested by the way he looked at me, and I sure was interested in him. The problem was that JD was engaged to Helen Hensley, a match that had been arranged by their families. I became engaged to his cousin, Jake Dale, just to spite JD, although I had no intention of marrying Jake.

Then, one night, Fate, which I now see brought me back to Tennessee in the first place, took another turn in my direction. I was angry at Jake Dale because he went out celebrating our engagement with the boys, and was drinking beer, and forgot about a date with me. He was trying to get back in my good graces as he walked me home from church along the country road leading to Bonnie's house. I kept telling him to go away, and leave me alone. We were right in front of the Kimsey house, which was set somewhat back from the road. It was very dark, and we didn't know that JD was sitting on the porch, listening to us argue.

Suddenly, JD stepped out of the shadows, took Jake by the arm, and told him to leave. He said, "I'll take Katherine home." Jake turned on his heel and stalked off.

JD walked me to Bonnie's house, and we sat on the porch swing, talking until almost midnight. He told me I was beautiful, and he had fallen in love with me the first time he saw me. I asked him why he had never paid any attention to me, and he said he figured that when I got done with the rest of the boys, I would get around to him. JD said he would break his engagement to Helen if I would break my engagement to Jake. I told him I already had; that was why Jake and I were arguing.

That night was December 7, 1938. On a cold, rainy night, a little over a month later, January 17, 1939, JD and I eloped across the Georgia state line in his old Ford. We had the Justice of the Peace who had performed the marriage ceremony of a girlfriend of mine, and a witness he provided, sit in the back seat of the car, so they couldn't see, in the dark, how young I was. JD and I repeated our vows from the front seat, with rain seeping in through the car roof. We went to a movie afterwards.

Whoever married JD Kimsey was fated to live a different kind of life than the other girls in town. By a stroke of luck, it was I. We ended up living all over the world, having many different experiences in different cultures before JD retired. That's not to say that things were always easy. When we got married, the country was still reeling from The Great Depression, and it was hard for young men to get work. JD had only a high school education, plus a couple of college business courses, taken by correspondence. He got work in a saw mill at first, and then did farm work for $1.00 a day.

Shortly after our first child, Brenda, was born in February, 1940, JD heard that Utah Construction Company was hiring men for a tunnel job in Andrews, North Carolina. JD made 13 trips to Andrews, trying to get hired, before Ben Arp, the project manager, gave him a job operating a drill. JD didn't know how to drill, but his father told him what to do, and he was a foreman within three months.

We had had two more children, Carolyn and Robert, by the time we moved permanently from Tennessee the summer of 1946. We then lived in the western part of the United States while JD worked for Ben Arp on various underground construction jobs. Ben promoted him to general superintendent in 1948 when he went to work on a tunnel project for Utah Construction in Bingham Canyon, Utah. In 1951, our last child, Richard, was born in Salt Lake City.

In 1956, Ben Arp called JD and said FASMA, a French-American company, was looking for someone to oversee the completion of a dam and underground power station as part of the Snowy Mountains Project in Australia; that they were so far behind, they were about to lose the contract. He had recommended JD for the job. A Frenchman came to Salt Lake City to negotiate with JD, and a deal was struck.

After that, we spent over 20 years living in foreign countries, while JD worked as the project manager on various jobs. We loved Australia the most. We lived there for 12 years on three different assignments. The Australian people were very friendly to Americans. We met Prime Minister Robert Menzies when he came to visit the job site, and I helped give a tea for his wife, Dame Pattie. We entertained the French Ambassador and other dignitaries.

While managing an important project when we lived in New Zealand, JD appeared with Prime Minister Keith Jacka Holyoake on the cover of *Photo Review*, a New Zealand news magazine. By then, JD had a reputation as one of the top underground construction men in the world. We also lived in Greece and Chile, and JD traveled to other countries in the course of his employment.

As is customary in the construction business, JD's company paid all of our housing expenses when we lived overseas. They paid first-class airfare or ship accommodations for us when we traveled between the United States and foreign countries. They paid for our vacation trips home. When local schools were not adequate, and it became necessary to send our two youngest children to board at a private high school in the United States, the company paid for this as well.

JD and I faced heartaches and tragedies over the years just like every other couple, but all in all, we had a wonderful life together, and we ended up financially secure in our retirement from his hard work. The example he set influenced our children, all of whom became successful adults.

If it had not been for Beryl giving me the sapphire ring, and Bonnie coming to Canton to take me back to Turtletown, I would not have met JD, and I would have missed a great adventure. My daughter Brenda asked me recently what happened to the sapphire ring and Beryl Hall. I still had the sapphire ring, and wore it some, even after JD and I got married, but it was stolen many years ago. It truly was only a friendship ring as far as I was concerned. But, Beryl Hall never did get married.

By Katherine O'Neal Kimsey

Katherine O'Neal Kimsey is an artist of still life and landscapes. She has a home in Scottsdale, Arizona, where she lives near her daughter, Brenda, "the "best son-in-law in the world," and their family. She enjoys writing poetry and received a Golden Poet award from the World of Poetry in 1988 for her poem "The Torrent," written under her pen name Ramona See. Katy, now a widow, says she still misses Australia and other countries she lived in when her husband, JD, worked on overseas jobs. She enjoys frequent visits to Coronado, California, during the hot weather in Arizona, and also travels frequently to Utah to see her other children and grandchildren.

Mother's Voice

I grew up "on the fence," as we say in the Missouri Ozarks. Some people believe in extrasensory perception. Others dismiss it with bemused tolerance or persecution.

Many families in my community still believe in haunted houses and "bright, round moving objects high up in the sky." Most look upon these people as "odd." I wonder, are they?

My father was a farmer who traveled around investing in livestock and real estate. Many times, I heard him say that his subconscious, or intuition, often warned him not to travel, or told him to buy or sell, or not to buy or sell, something, and the advice turned out to be right.

Are we so set in our ways that we can't understand or accept anything except what can be seen by the naked eye, or recorded on tape by the human voice?

I had an experience that will always be a wonderment to me.

My mother had a stroke and could not talk. My father kept her at home and had nurses with her round the clock. He also hired a speech teacher to work with her.

My husband, Glenn, and I lived 100 miles to the east of my parents' house. Three times a week, after the school bell rang at 3:00 p.m., I left my classroom and drove to Doniphan, Missouri, to be with Mother, and try to keep up her morale.

Teaching school and traveling 100 miles to my parents' home, and then driving the 100 miles back to our home in Cape Girardeau, meant that I was always short of sleep.

One evening in May, 1983, I bid Mother goodbye, hugged my father, then headed the car for Cape Girardeau to meet Glenn.

I had been on the road about an hour. Suddenly, Mother yelled, "Garnet!" I awoke. The car was headed straight for a bridge rail and pillar. I slammed on the brakes and swerved the car away from the railing. I stopped. My hands shook on the steering wheel. My feet trembled on the floorboard. Shivering from head to foot, every organ inside me yo-yoed up and down. I stayed parked for what seemed like an eternity.

Where did Mother's voice come from? It had been in the car. How did Mother know I had gone to sleep? I had left my parents' home an hour before.

Was I hearing Mother's voice from my subconscious mind? How come Mother yelled at me just as my car was heading for the bridge? I didn't know!

I had fallen asleep; Mother's voice had awakened me. I was scared; frightened that I had almost hit the bridge, and shocked at hearing Mother's voice.

When I got home, I telephoned my father. The first thing he said was, "Your mother spoke. She called 'Garnet' and sat up in bed. You had been gone about an hour."

That was right around the time I almost hit the bridge!

Through chattering teeth, I told my father about falling asleep while driving, and how Mother's crying out had probably saved my life.

Father told me he had had many experiences in his life when some unknown power had warned him of danger. He told me about some of the incidents, and that began to calm me, but I still had not regained my composure. I asked my father to tell Mother that I heard her call my name.

When I got home, I told Glenn about hearing Mother's voice and said, "You probably don't believe me."

"Garnet, I believe you," he said. "I could tell you of many incidents during World War II when the men in my squadron heard unknown voices or felt an unknown power. The reason I've never mentioned these things before is because many people aren't ready to hear about extrasensory powers."

My talk with Glenn helped relieve some of my tension. I didn't fully comprehend how I had heard Mother speak. From the time she had her stroke, until she died 15 months later, *my name,* on that near fatal day, was the only word or time anyone heard her speak.

A Fate beyond my control decided what was to happen to me that day. After that, I was humble when I heard people speak about "strange" happenings in their lives. This occasion made me give credence to guardian angels and heavenly spirits.

I was in danger; Mother's voice saved me.

By Garnet Hunt White

Garnet Hunt White is a retired schoolteacher who wrote stories using her pupil's names in order to encourage them to read. Garnet has been published in two anthologies, *Stories for a Woman's Heart* and *Chocolate for a Chocolate Lover's Heart.* Several of her stories have won awards, and she organized the Ripley

County Writers Guild in Missouri where she lives. She loves animals, as did her late, wonderful husband, Glenn.

The Wig

Our hiking group met at Starbucks in Scottsdale at 8:00 a.m. that Sunday. We were headed for the Tonto National Forest for a hike in the Salome Creek Wilderness, northeast of Theodore Roosevelt Lake. Our hiking leader, Richard Allen, estimated it would take about two hours to get to the trail head. We had 20 hikers and six vehicles. Some people double up and ride together when we go on our hiking trips—but my husband, Dick, and I always drive alone, so we can leave for home whenever we want to, without inconveniencing anyone else.

It was a beautiful drive through the Arizona desert on a mid-March morning. With the recent rains, the sagebrush and other shrubs and grasses were green, and the spring wildflowers were beginning to bloom. Already, a profusion of gold and purple flowers were showing off alongside the road, creeping out into the desert and chasing each other up the lower mountain slopes.

One of the places we drove past was the town of Punkin Center, where my former piano teacher had moved probably 12 years before to live near her cousin, and I said to Dick that on the way back, I would like to stop and look her up, if it wasn't too late in the day. He asked, "How would you find her?" but *I just knew* I would, and answered confidently, "Oh, it would be easy because Punkin Center is so small, and her cousin owned a store there." Punkin Center, originally founded in 1945 as a weather station, is part of the Tonto Basin area.

I was having a mental block as I tried to remember my piano teacher's name. I wanted to say Eilene, but I knew that was wrong, and something like Thomas was coming to mind for her last name, but I knew that was wrong, too. I had never known her age, but she was fairly old, and always dressed up, with a too-large brown wig that reminded me of a hornet's nest, slightly askew and falling over one eye, seemingly blocking her vision.

I remembered being very upset when she announced she was moving after I had taken piano lessons from her for several years. Not only was I quite fond of her, but I knew I would have trouble finding another piano teacher who would accommodate her schedule to my crazy work hours as a lawyer. And, I was right. When she moved, it was basically the end of my piano instruction.

Now, we left Route 85, a few miles before Roosevelt Lake, taking a dirt road cut-off that would lead us 17 miles around the northern end of the lake to the trail head. Just after we got off the main highway, we came to a large "Road Closed" barrier. We couldn't understand why there would be a road closure, and thought that perhaps someone had forgotten the barrier was there, so we cautiously went around it. A short distance ahead, we saw what the problem was—the road crossed a wash, and the wash had water running through it at least two-feet deep.

Some of the hikers wanted to drive on, but Richard Allen was concerned that even deeper water might lay ahead from recent rains. He suggested that we abandon our plans to hike to the Salome Creek Wilderness area and go to Four Peaks instead, another nearby wilderness area where we could take a hiking trail with which he was more familiar. When we got to the Four Peaks area, we could see that the mountains still had snow in the upper elevations, so we agreed we would drive to the trail head, but if we ran into snow, we would just eat our lunches and head back home.

The dirt road to the Four Peaks trail head was one lane, twisting and turning up the rugged mountain. Dick hugged the inside of the mountain as he drove, while I looked off the steep cliff on my right to the desert foothills below. The rapid change in altitude was making me woozy. Scared to death our van would go off the side of this steep, narrow road, I suddenly insisted in a loud voice that I just couldn't take any more. After a particularly hair-raising bend, Dick stopped, managed to get the van turned around at a cut-out, and headed back down the mountain. When we got to a viewpoint where we could pull off and park, we ate our sandwiches, and then left for home, stopping to buy gas along the highway.

As we came to Punkin Center, I said, "Let's stop and say hello to my piano teacher." Realizing that I was serious, Dick pulled off the main highway to take the bypass through town, saying in a puzzled tone, "I don't know where to look." Since it was Sunday, the post office and most of the stores were closed, but as we were driving down the road through a hodge podge of buildings, off to our left, I saw a trading post up on a slight rise, set back maybe 50 yards from the road, just before a large embankment blocked my view. I said somewhat nonchalantly, "Oh, that must have been my piano teacher's cousin's store we just passed; I spotted my piano teacher's wig."

Dick gave me an incredulous look and a "Huh?" but he backed up, and pulled the van up the rise to the front of the store. I jumped out. Sure enough, it *was* my piano teacher, who had just closed the trading post for the day and was walking to her home, which was about 60 yards away. She was extremely surprised, but immediately recognized us, and invited us in to see her very nice home, where she served us mango juice and cookies, and we got all caught up on what had happened in each other's lives in the years since she had moved from Scottsdale. She had taught one of my sons piano, too, and I had the pleasure of telling her he was now married with two young children. As we visited, I finally remembered her name: Irene Thompson.

How *I just knew* that I would find Irene if we went to Punkin Center in search of her that day is a mystery. Fate took a sequence of synchronized steps to arrive at this harmonious outcome.

It was only because Irene left the trading post exactly when she did, and we arrived there exactly when we did, that I saw her. If we had arrived a few minutes earlier, like if we hadn't stopped for gas on the highway, she still would have been inside the trading post when we drove by, and I honestly had no way of knowing the trading post was the store owned by her cousin until I saw Irene walking away from it as we drove by.

If we had driven by a few seconds later than we did, I would not have seen her because she already would have walked behind the embankment that blocked the view from the road, and a minute or two later, she would have been inside her house. Since I could not remember her name, there was no way I could have tried to locate her by asking any passersby if they knew her.

And, I would not have realized that the woman I saw from the road, in the quick second before my view was blocked, was my teacher, either—except for the wig! You couldn't miss the wig! Irene did tell us she was 91, and slightly hard of hearing, but otherwise seemed spry and doing fine.

When we got home, Dick sent Richard Allen an e-mail, telling him what had happened to us. We received an e-mail back the next morning that read:

> Dear Dick and Brenda: I'm glad things worked out OK for you. Actually, that bend was the worst place in the road. It got better after that. From the top, you can see Phoenix in the distance. I got the message that you had stopped. Thanks for being such good sports about all the changes of plans, etc. Nice that you could run into the teacher—maybe it was meant to be! Richard

Yes, maybe it was meant to be. I can always go on another hike, but who knows if I ever would have seen my piano teacher again if we had continued on our way to the Four Peaks trail head. And seeing her was indeed a pleasant, nostalgic experience for me.

As we go down the highway of life with incidents taking place, seemingly at random, "Fate" happens in a way we can't always explain.

By Brenda Warneka

A Life-Altering Twist of Fate

Things that happen in real life are sometimes much beyond any imagination and fiction.

In December 1941, in the city of Simferopol in the former Soviet Union, Tatiana Zelenskaya, a singer, and her husband, Pavel Chariuta, the musician who accompanied her, were young actors performing together on stage. The city was already under Nazi rule when one of the theater employees approached Tatiana with a request that would save a life and forever change the lives of the young couple.

The employee, whom Tatiana would later realize had heard of the German plans via his connection with the municipal underground, asked if she would take in and hide a Jewish child. He informed her that in just a few days all the Jews in the city would be gathered in one location prior to their deportation. At the collection point it would be possible, in the general confusion, to "steal" a few children, and by so doing, to save them, he confided.

In spite of the danger, Tatiana agreed, and on the appointed day and time she stood in a nearby alley leading to the designated collection point of the Jews and waited. After some time, a stranger appeared leading a little girl with black, curly hair and big, frightened eyes by the hand. The woman handed her charge to Tatiana who walked home with the child through the city's alleys and back streets. As Tatiana took off the little girl's coat, a note, with the child's name, address, and date of birth fell to the floor.

From that day on, four-year-old Luba Kogan lived in Tatiana and Pavel's home. At first, she was sad, refused to eat and constantly asked, "Where is my mother?" Weeks passed, and slowly Luba's memories of her past life faded and were replaced with new impressions, until one day she referred to Tatiana as "Mother." It was not long before Tatiana and Pavel became extremely attached to Luba and could not imagine life without her.

Although it was illegal to harbor a Jewish child and the neighbors were well aware of Luba, not a single one of them questioned her origins or disclosed her presence during the two years and two months of the war.

Years later, when Tatiana herself was questioned as to whether she was frightened to hide a Jewish child, she replied, "I was young...I did what I felt I had to do. My parents told me that I was jeopardizing myself, but my husband supported me."

Following the war, the couple attempted to determine the fate of Luba's parents. Through the Kogan family's neighbors, they learned that Luba's mother and brother had been executed and that her father died while serving on the front.

In 1947, a man who introduced himself as a representative of the Jewish community approached the couple with an offer of monetary assistance towards Luba's care. Tatiana and Pavel refused for fear that if they accepted aid, Luba would be taken from them.

Luba continued to live with the couple well into adolescence without knowing that Tatiana and Pavel were not her biological parents. In 1953, when Luba was 16 years old and was required to obtain an identity card, Tatiana finally told her the true story of her childhood, and only then did Tatiana and Pavel officially adopt Luba.

In 1965, when Luba was already married and herself a mother, a coincidental meeting resulted in a startling turn of events. Luba's husband, a taxi driver, met another taxi driver, an older man, with a story to tell. As the younger man listened to the details which seemed to match the details of his wife's life, he came to the uncertain, but intuitive conclusion that this man might be Luba's biological father, who until then had been presumed dead in battle.

As it turned out, after the war, when Itzak Kogan, Luba's father, returned to Simferopol, following his service in the Red Army, his neighbors informed him that his wife and his two children had been killed. Overwhelmed by his loss, Itzak could not continue to live in Simferopol and therefore moved to Krasnodar in Russia. In time, Itzak remarried, started a new family, and began working as a taxi driver.

Following this encounter with Luba's husband that seemed more miracle than sheer coincidence, father and daughter were reunited in an emotional meeting that was reported by the local newspaper.

Many years later, following the deaths of both Pavel and Itzak, Luba brought Tatiana, the woman who saved her life and adopted her as her own child, to live with her. In 1993, one of Luba's sons immigrated to Israel with his family. While visiting Yad Vashem for the first time, her son learned of Yad Vashem's Righteous Among the Nations Department and told his mother's story to its staff members. In 1995, Tatiana Zelenskaya and Pavel Chariuta received the Righteous Among the Nations designation at a ceremony at Yad Vashem.

During the ceremony, Tatiana recalled the bittersweet twist of fate in a hushed voice and with tears in her eyes, said: "I remember that fall evening in 1941 when 15,000 Jews were murdered and how happy I was that I was able to save one life—that of a little girl who is standing next to me today—my beloved and only daughter."

That same year, Luba, her family, and Tatiana Zelenskaya immigrated to Israel where they are still living together today.

By Katia Gusarov

Katia Gusarov migrated from Russia to Israel in 1990. She became acquainted with Tatyana Zelenskaya and her adopted daughter Lyuba through her work for Yad Vashem, which is a huge complex outside of Jerusalem dedicated to the memory of the Holocaust (see www.yad-vashem.org.il). Katia works for the "Righteous Among the Nations" department, which is dedicated to gathering information and honoring non-Jews who rescued Jews, during World War II, at the risk of their own lives. The mother of three, Katia maintains friendly relations with Tatyana and Lyuba.

Her Brother's Keeper

I do not believe that the Good Lord plays dice.

—Albert Einstein

It was dusk, a beautiful evening. The setting sun filled the sky with streaks of orange and red. My girlfriend and I sat on a wooden bench overlooking the waterfall garden that was surrounded by pines and maples. The bench was on a 50-foot ridge where the waterfalls began. It was so perfect!

After an hour elapsed, we walked from the waterfall garden down the prairie grass slope. Then something very strange happened! On the way down the 40-degree incline, my equilibrium became a little shaky. As we all tend to do, I denied any problem and hoped it would go away. I was floating on air anyway, without a care in the world. Good job; promising future; beautiful, smart girlfriend; my parents were away on vacation; and my older sister, Brenda, was at her weekend job. All kinds of exciting images danced in my head!

Well, that night turned out to be the last night I was ever "without a care in the world," because at 11:30 p.m., long after I drove my girlfriend home, I awoke from a deep sleep with a severe headache. I ran downstairs to the kitchen and swallowed two Bufferin, thinking that was all I needed. Then I went down to the basement to rest on a cot, where I often sprawled out when I was under the weather, hoping the headache would dissipate. It persisted. I went back upstairs to the kitchen and called my friend Paul, who lived a few blocks away. Before I finished dialing his number, the headache became so severe that I curled up on the kitchen floor.

The next thing I knew, my sister, Brenda, was at my side. In a quivering voice, I told her of my problem. We lived only a few blocks from a hospital, so Brenda called the emergency room and told them she was bringing me in.

Brenda was the head choreographer at a dinner-theater, and that night, she was conducting a rehearsal for the musical, *The Best Little Whorehouse in Texas*. Opening night was just around the corner. Since the rehearsals often ran late into the night, Brenda usually took advantage of one of her perks, a rented hotel room, to avoid the late-night 40-minute drive home.

To make a long and excruciatingly painful story short, it turned out that my blinding headache, as well as the shaky equilibrium I had experienced earlier in the evening, were symptoms of a malignant brain tumor. Now, years later (thanks to extensive life-threatening surgery, and many, many prayers), I am cancer free.

My sister often recollects that on July 16, 1990, the evening of my admittance to the hospital, she was tired after the long rehearsal and was seriously considering staying overnight at the resort. But, a *warning* in her mind made her go home; she had a feeling that something was terribly wrong.

If Brenda had not heard, and responded to that inner message, the doctors said, I probably would have gone into a coma and died. I wouldn't be here to hug her today!

By Darryl C. Didier

Adapted with permission from *Force A Miracle* by Darryl C. Didier. Copyright©2000. All rights reserved.

Darryl C. Didier is flourishing after undergoing a very complicated, life-threatening brain tumor operation. Following a year of intensive rehabilitation, Darryl became actively involved with his local chapter of the American Cancer Society by raising funds, and as a motivational speaker at grade schools, high schools, businesses, and even a prison. He walks, he talks, he does everything he did before his surgery. The only difference is that he no longer takes life for granted—not for a single moment. His recent book, *Force a Miracle,* with a Forward by Mike Ditka, Hall of Fame football player, is an inspiration, as is Darryl, to anyone who has a hurdle to climb.

Swimmer's Delight

My hometown, Corning, California, basted like a well-done chicken in 100 degree heat that August morning. Dad had decided to go fishing on the Sacramento River, and we four kids were excited to accompany him. We would play at the swimming hole, known as Swimmer's Delight, while he fished. This was when I was eleven years old, many years before the Whiskytown Dam was built and made the river too cold and deep for swimming.

Ten miles from home, we crossed over Woodson's Bridge to the picnic grounds, and parked our car. Huge oak trees trailing long vines cast cooling shade over the picnic tables. We kids loved to seize a wrist-thick vine, and with a running start, swing out over the water and drop into the river with a huge splash.

Mom was adamant about doing our swimming before we ate. No one seemed too concerned about the river's current while we swam in the green water. Oh, what bliss!

We dove and swam all afternoon, coming out now and then to bask on the hot sand and rocks. The beach made a wide sweeping curve at that spot. From there, I could see my dad, made smaller by the distance, standing in a rowboat borrowed from his friend Charlie Hansen. Earlier, I had seen Charlie visiting with friends in the park near the picnic tables.

Dad's fishing line made little rainbows of light now and again as he cast into the water. My mouth watered, savoring the thought of the 18-inch black bass we would have for supper. Dad always caught something.

My perfect day was shattered by two men on the bridge, hollering and waving their arms like crazy men, pointing down into the river. I could tell they were hoboes by the packs on their shoulders: men who rode the trains from town to town looking for work, or maybe, because they just wanted to roam. We kids had been strictly warned to stay away from them.

The hoboes kept yelling and pointing until men lounging on the river bank stood up to see what all the commotion was about. Two of them dove into the river, their arms flaying the water into a froth as they swam, nearly going under the bridge. They came back, each stroking with one arm, towing a body between them. As they came ashore, we could see it was a boy, his arms dangling, his head hanging down, his feet leaving wet lines as he was dragged across the sand. His two rescuers rushed him to one of the picnic tables.

It was my nine-year old brother, Floyd! I was petrified with fear, until someone yelled, "Go get Mike!" Mike was my father. I set out, running barefoot across the hot rocks along the shore, my arms pumping up and down, my legs churning, jumping over knee-high rocks, until I was close to my dad's fishing grounds.

I yelled, "Daddy, Floyd drowned. Hurry! Hurry!" I cupped my hands and screamed at him, over and over. I saw him throw down his rod, sit to grasp the oars and pull downriver with all his might. I ran back, but my dad beat me to the site.

When I arrived, out of breath, frantic with fear, Charlie Hansen lay on the picnic table, using his body as a log, while my father rolled and squeezed Floyd's body across Charlie's, over and over. As I watched Floyd's limp body being pummeled, all I could think of was that I had brought this terrible tragedy on our family because in my angry quarreling with Floyd that morning, I had yelled, "I wish you were dead!" Now, he was lying motionless, making no response to the efforts to revive him. I wasn't aware of it, but Mom later said that I was crying and promising never to fight with Floyd, or anyone else, again if God would only let him live.

All at once, water gushed from Floyd's mouth, and he stirred. I don't recall what else happened, but I remember my brother, sitting up, wheezing for breath while people around us laughed with relief, and whacked my father on the back, everyone talking at once. In time, humbled and contrite, I looked unsuccessfully for the two hoboes. I wanted to thank them for saving my brother's life by their persistent yelling and pointing.

The two men who rescued Floyd said that when they reached him, they had caught him by his swimming trunks, just as he was going under a pile of brush at the river's bottom. Had they been even a second later, they would have missed him. The two hoboes, looking down from the bridge, had seen Floyd drifting downstream with the current. Another fortunate thing was that Floyd had swallowed his tongue, which kept water out of his lungs. When my father used a finger to clear Floyd's mouth of debris, it loosened his tongue and enabled him to cough up water he had gulped in.

We never knew who the two hoboes were, or why they were on the bridge that day. No one saw them again. I hope they know that they saved my brother's life.

I often wonder: If those hoboes had taken a different route, what would have happened to my brother? No one else was on the bridge that afternoon. And what if the two men who dove into the river had stayed home? Floyd said only the other day, "Sometimes I think of my war buddies who didn't make it home. Why was I spared?"

By Virginia K. Sparks

Virginia Kennedy Sparks grew up in Corning, California, attending local schools. After moving to Humboldt County, California, she wrote historical pieces for the *Humboldt Times,* and later wrote a column on historical subjects for the *Humboldt Beacon.* Her writing has appeared in various magazines and historical quarterlies. Other interests include sewing, gardening and landscaping, recipes from the 1700s and 1800s, photography and genealogy. She also enjoys volunteering at the library.

Pop's Angel Lounge

When Pop remodeled our home, he added what each member of the family wanted—two extra bedrooms, an additional bath, a larger kitchen, a breakfast nook, a sun porch and thirty-two windows. However, after the renovation, one room in the middle of the house was left with no windows. We called it the "dark room."

When I was a child, chills raced up and down my spine every time I walked into the dark room. Who knew what could be hiding in the shadows? Vicky, one of my sixth grade classmates, thought she saw a ghost in the room. Two other friends, Stella and Ora, were afraid to go into the room at all. My parents built a new home the year I was married, and they decided to sell the house with the dark room. My husband, Glenn, and I bought it. We used the dark room only as a hall and never tarried in passing between rooms. I still thought of the room with apprehension.

Glenn's job took him out of town two nights each week. I stayed home with our dog, Rex. Late one night when Glenn was away, a rainstorm knocked out the lights. Rex jumped on my bed and barked until I awoke. He then whined and ran around the room every time the lightning flashed or the thunder clapped.

I finally got out of bed and took Rex to the dark room. He felt safe there because he couldn't see the lightning or hear the thunder. As we lay on the floor, huddled together, I dropped off to sleep.

Rex suddenly started to yelp again. He tugged on my sleeve, bounded out of the room, ran toward the bedroom door, then back to me, only to repeat his antics.

What did I smell? What was that flashing yellow light? I stumbled toward the bedroom. Flames covered my bed! Lightning had run into the house and ignited the bed covers. I grabbed Glenn's pillow. Clutching it with both hands, I began beating out the blaze. Adrenaline was flowing through my body. I kept slamming the pillow onto the blaze, pounding until the fire was ash.

With the fire out, my body went limp. The storm still raged. I dropped to the floor and crawled toward the dark room. Rex kept howling, but he nudged me along. Finally, sprawled on the floor in the dark room, I hugged him.

When the morning calmness came, I realized I had spent more time in the dark room that night than in all the times I had been there in the past.

I put breakfast on hold, petted Rex, and said, "Gotta call Mom and Pop to see if they're O.K. Then I'll fix you some chicken strips."

A dead telephone. The storm had knocked out my phone line. I put Rex into the car to go to my parents' house. But before I got out of the garage, their car pulled into the driveway.

I jumped out of the car and ran to them, jabbering and crying.

"Hey, hey!" Pop said. "Are you all right? Can't understand a word you're saying. Glenn called. Said he couldn't get through to you."

Grinning through tears, I embraced them both. Inside the house, I showed them the bedroom. Then, half-laughing, half-crying, I led them into the dark room to finish the tale of how Pop, Rex, and the dark room saved my life.

"Oh, Pop. I'm so thankful to you for this room," I sobbed as he put his arms around me. "I'm alive now because of you."

Ever since then, I have had new respect for Pop's dark room. He built an Angels' Lounge.

By Garnet Hunt White

The Fate of Aspirin

When you turn the right corner, at just the right time, in just the right place,
and meet just the right circumstances, person or event...you come to know
the true meaning of fate.

I wasn't even supposed to be there. I was graduating from college, and the gang at my second job, a local restaurant in town, wanted to throw me a congratulatory party.

"We'll meet you at the Raw Bar," they shouted on my way out the door with a tip-apron full of extra singles from an impromptu collection they'd taken up for me. "Don't be late!"

Of course, with my college-boy sense of direction, I went to the Raw Bar on the south side of town, even as they all sped directly to the north one. Now, a full hour later, and still nursing my lukewarm first beer of the night, I had finally gotten a bartender at the *other* Raw Bar to summon the most sober of the group to the bar phone. Needless to say, the party had been a roaring success, and none of them were in any condition to come and meet me.

I sat back down on my warm bar stool and finished my beer. "Oh well," I thought to myself, rising to leave, "at least I won't have a hangover tomorrow."

At that moment, the gorgeous teacher from the school where I had just completed my student internship walked through the door with a friend of hers. Embarrassed to be caught in a dingy bar all alone, I quickly turned to the bartender and ordered another beer.

Meanwhile, the long-legged beauty I had lusted after, day in and day out, strode effortlessly to a table for two and joined her friend for a pitcher of beer and some steamed shrimp. I watched from behind the camouflage of my 300-pound biker barstool neighbor as the teacher's delicate hands alternately sipped at her frothy beer and peeled a still steaming shrimp.

How different she seemed from the consummate teacher who had often written me "helpful" little notes after witnessing yet another disastrous attempt on my part to take my unruly 5th grade class through the elementary school halls quietly.

"If you divided your line in half," she had written in elegant script on floral stationary, "they'd be much easier to control. Sincerely, Ms. Richard." I'd saved every note and devoured them as religiously as I did my college advisor's half-hearted yet stern evaluations.

And now she was *here*, live and in person. My stressful senior internship, leading to my teaching degree, was over. There would be no more little notes from "Ms. Richard." No more expert advice in the teachers' lounge while I secretly vibed her with sexy ESP and suggestive, rapid eye movements. But it didn't matter anyway. My flirtations had gone unrequited, and the other bachelors at the bar already were making plans to swoop in on the two unescorted beauties and their half-eaten shrimp.

I slid my half-empty beer and a hefty tip across the bar and left without a word. The humidity in the warm Florida night air reminded me of the dull headache forming in the back of my weary head, and I drove my battered Corolla to the brightly-lit gas station across the street. Inside, I grabbed a Diet Coke and a single packet of aspirin before returning to my car.

Across the street lay the salty, weathered Raw Bar with all of its life preservers and fake crab-covered glory. I sipped at my soda greedily and felt the night's tension lighten and my headache disappear. Stowing the bright yellow packet in my pocket, I sat in my idling car and wondered why I hadn't stayed. Why hadn't I at least tried to make pleasant conversation and get to know her away from school? I'd never see her again anyway. What did I have to lose?

Finishing my soda, I returned to my old parking space and strode back into the Raw Bar confidently. Well…all right, but…at least I walked back in! I ordered a pitcher of light beer (I was guessing that is what she would like) and with trembling hands, brought it and a clean glass over to Ms. Richard's table. She seemed surprised to see me, and my heart fluttered as she rose to greet me.

"Thanks for the offer," she replied as I hefted the sweaty pitcher of beer. "But maybe you and Cheryl can enjoy it. I was just leaving…I've got this nasty headache." Sure, it could have been a line, but she *was* rubbing her temples rather vigorously.

Just then, the crisp, yellow packet in my pocket called out to me, and I snatched it up, ripped it open and deposited two aspirin into her warm, soft hand.

Her eyes lit up and she swallowed them with a sip of fresh beer.

"Gee," she said with a smile she'd never revealed on the school grounds, "suddenly I feel a whole lot better!"

I've often looked back on that night in utter amazement. So many things seemed to align…in just the right order. What if I'd gone to the "right" Raw Bar? What if I'd never bought that aspirin? What if I'd gone home instead of coming back? What if she had left before I got back? What if she preferred Tylenol?

Oh well, I guess I've had plenty of time to ponder those questions. Ms. Richard and I have been happily married for nine years.

By Rusty Fischer

Rusty Fischer is a magazine editor and free-lance writer. He finds that he keeps coming back to the same subject matter: his beautiful wife. If it's true that you should only write about what you know, then he knows that their love is the best material a writer could ever find! He and his wife, Martha, a talented singer, enjoy walking, eating out, going to movies and traveling.

The Hand of Destiny

When my Canadian husband died, after 31 happily married years, I was trying to run a miniature farm. We also owned a small, one-bedroom apartment that we used when in town, the big city of San Paulo, Brazil.

Colin's estate was not very extensive, but he had willed it all to me, since we had no children. It should have been a simple matter, but I needed a lawyer. A friend recommended one, and we started the legal work on the estate. I discovered later on that the lawyer I had chosen was going through a severe case of depression, and the proceedings took a long time. He had a young assistant who had just finished her training. She was 27, a tall, graceful girl, named Katia, and he began to leave the case more and more in her hands.

Brazilian inheritance laws are complex. Parents and children are "necessary heirs." Colin was 83, but the judge insisted that I provide proof of his parents' deaths. His father had died when Colin was 14, and his mother when he was in his twenties. Colin had left his native town, Vancouver, British Columbia, forty years earlier, and I found nothing in his papers concerning his parents' deaths. His naturalization papers said he had no parents living, and our wedding certificate made it quite clear that they were deceased. But the judge insisted on death certificates, and it took Katia and me about six months before I was able to get Colin's sister-in-law and one of my cousins, then a resident in Vancouver, to search the cemeteries until they found the graves. They then provided a certificate that both Mr. And Mrs. Macdonell had, in fact, been buried there, in Vancouver, half a century before.

During this time, I grew to depend on Katia for emotional support, and one day she introduced me to her mother, a small, very determined little person. A few weeks later, mother and daughter came to visit me in my apartment. The mother, Suzana, had given her apartment to Katia and her future husband, and they wanted to have it redecorated. Mother and daughter needed a place to live. Could they share my home with me until the wedding?

I agreed. I was lonely, and in any case, I spent most of my time out on the farm. The wedding took place ten months later, and I invited Suzana to go on living with me as long as she cared to. The young people could be on their own, although Suzana would still have a room at her old apartment.

So far, there was nothing unusual about a widow coming to share a home with her lawyer's mother. This could happen to anyone. But one day, at breakfast, Suzana and I were talking about my farm, and I commented on her understanding of my difficulties in running it.

"I ought to know something about country life. I was born on a farm and lived there until I was eight years old," she said.

"Where was it?"

"It was near Santa Cruz do Rio Pardo."

"That's curious. My uncle Alfred had a farm there. He was drowned in the Rio Pardo, when I was nine years old, and his widow took her children back to England."

Suzana's eyes opened wide, and she shivered.

"Then it was the same farm. My father was overseer there, and I often heard the story about the former owner, an Englishman, who was drowned when his car slid off the river barge."

I shivered, too. I had troubled memories of Auntie Ruth staying in our home before she returned to England, to raise five children on her own.

There are 12 million people in Sao Paulo, and tens of thousands of lawyers. Suzana and I still share the same apartment and all of life's ups and downs. We feel we were destined to meet.

By Julia Macdonell

Julia Macdonell is a second-generation Brazilian, whose British and American grandparents came to Brazil in the late 19th century. She grew up in a bilingual home and attended an American grade and high school. She worked as a bilingual secretary-translator and, for 15 years, taught English in an accredited language school. She is an avid student of Brazilian history and folklore, and in recent years, following a childhood dream, is taking writing courses and participating in writers' groups. She wishes to record both the legends of the countryside and the experiences of a lifetime.

What Is Fate?

Fate happens to me on a regular basis. I need something and it happens. I think of someone, and they call. I pride myself on what others see as simply a coincidence. To me, it is a sign that I am on the true path to my authentic self and that I am living my destiny. I strive to make fate my reality, and life is a quiet thing.

Amy Casey (actress, singer)

Taxi Driver's Passenger Is His Long-Lost Son

A taxi driver found the son he last saw 34 years ago—as a fare in the back of his cab. The chance reunion came when Barry Bagshaw, 61, picked up a fare at a motel near Brighten in southern England. A short time into the journey, the woman accompanying the man in the back spotted the driver's identity badge and noticed he had the same surname as her boyfriend.

"The blood just drained out of me when he said, 'I'm your son,'" Barry told BBC radio. "I didn't recognize him at first. It certainly won't be another 34 years before I see him again."

His son, Colin, 39, a chef, who was about to leave the area for good, had thought his father was dead—even though they found they lived just streets apart.

Barry, who has another son and a daughter, lost touch with his children when his marriage broke down while he was serving in the army in Hong Kong.

The Emissary

Fate is an unexpected intervention by the Divine that often is considered to
be coincidence by mere mortals like us.

My sister was dying of cancer. I was very sad over her illness, but I had only to think of the constant anguish suffered by my parents, who were caring for her, to feel even sadder. "Get your affairs in order," the doctors had bluntly told her. "There is nothing that can be done. Maybe you have six months; maybe not." But my family does not dissuade easily. My father, who was a cross between an ill-tempered grizzly and a lovable koala, began to assemble the considerable financial resources necessary to pay for an experimental bone marrow transplant. In 1990, when this happened, such a procedure was considered miraculous if it allowed a patient to survive more than a year or so.

One afternoon, I found myself in an uncomfortable social setting. I did not know most of the people who were there. The topic that occupied our conversation was personal tragedy. Great, I thought. Just the thing to cheer me up.

A young woman was leading the conversation. She looked vaguely familiar, but I certainly did not know her. Lanky and slightly awkward, she was the kind of utterly common girl who would normally escape one's notice. Even her name was extraordinarily commonplace: Mary. As she spoke, though, it was obvious there was something unusual about her. She'd had a dream, she said. A very young baby was critically ill and the child's doctors had used all the medical magic they could muster. It was just a matter of time. The dream was so real, she told us; it consumed her thoughts. She could see every feature of the baby—her face, her smile, the details of the yellow dress she wore. Mary said she was convinced a real baby existed—this baby—who was somewhere dying, and she could not ignore the dream any longer. She called a network of her friends and told them of her dream, and she insisted they had to pray for the baby. And so they did.

Some weeks later, Mary continued, an old friend invited her to see her new home. The two women had not seen each other for years. When she arrived, her friend radiated delight and happiness. There was the new home of which she was so proud, but mostly she had a surprise for Mary, and that was the real reason behind the invitation. The surprise: to show Mary her new baby girl. "We call her our 'Miracle Baby,'" the mother glowed, handing her to Mary. "The doctors had told us she would die; but she did not." Suddenly, Mary realized why her dream had been so powerful and her need to pray so intense: This was the sick baby of her dream—the Miracle Baby—now in her arms, wearing her new yellow Easter dress.

As we all began to leave our gathering later that afternoon, I had to seek out Mary. I needed her help for my sister. We spoke only for a few moments that afternoon. "My sister is terminal," I said. "I need your prayers, and the prayers of your friends." I could barely talk. A huge knot of emotion sat in my throat, and tears welled in my eyes. Yes, she said—very matter of factly—they would be happy to pray for her.

I felt a bit foolish. I had, after all, approached a perfect stranger and asked for a miracle, practically blubbering on my double-breasted suit in the process. A crazy continuum of feelings wandered through me as she walked away that after-noon: gullibility, relief, hope, stupidity. In the ensuing weeks, I looked for her at some of the places I thought she might frequent, but nothing. A few weeks went by. Then, as I was walking to a little delicatessen one day, Mary happened to see me coming down the street. She called me over.

"Oh, listen, I am glad I found you," she said, seemingly short of time. "Tell your sister a lot of us prayed for her. She is going to be fine. Her cancer is gone."

That was it. No big explanation of how she knew this; just, "Her cancer is gone."

Then she offered a little wave and departed as though we were old friends.

Eleven years have passed since that afternoon. To her doctors' amazement, my sister is alive today, and cancer free. She is not perfect; the bone marrow trans-plant left her with anemia, a compromised immune system and unrelenting fatigue. But she is alive and happy.

I am sure that most who hear this story will conclude that nothing more than coincidence was at work here. The transplant worked. Period. That is what they would say. But, that is an over-simplification of our world. Virtually all of the other women my sister met in the bone marrow unit that winter died long ago. She is one of just two survivors.

And Mary? I never did see Mary again. I have not seen her since that casual meeting on the street more than a decade ago. To be honest, I doubt that I would even recognize her. She was, after all, just a normal, lanky, awkward girl. A curious emissary of Fate.

By Sigfried Brian Barger

Siegfried Brian Barger lives in the Evergreen-Idaho Springs region of Colorado. He is an investment writer and stock market forecaster, who has written under the moniker MonyWolf. He is also a novelist and is very proud of his first published novel, *Fontana*.

Finding Daniel Joseph

Fate isn't a hurricane rushing in at 300 miles an hour, but a gentle push that gives us direction affecting events in our lives.

—Ronald Harmon

"'*Souleiado*'…[it's] one of those suitcase words with a ton of meaning packed into it," Miriam, the heroine of my time-travel novel, *Souleiado*, tells a new friend. She goes on to explain how that one little word translates roughly from the French as "the illumination created when the sun breaks through the clouds just after a rainstorm."

Miriam showed up in that room with all the interesting clutter that I call my imagination about a year after my husband Tim's death in a car accident. She had a lot of baggage with her, and you know, most of it looked a lot like mine. She, too, had been widowed suddenly and unexpectedly and was trying to piece together a new life for herself and her young daughter. She was an artist; I am a writer with closet-cartoonist tendencies whose reporter's notebook used to be covered with all these rat-like caricatures of people at town meetings I was covering. And she, like I, was having a number of other-worldly experiences that she couldn't explain away.

Most of the other characters and their names and quirks came to me easily enough. Miriam's husband, Jared, who remains a strong presence in the novel despite dying in the prologue, was clearly Tim, just as their intuitive little foot-in-both-worlds daughter was our Marissa. And all the secondary characters and even the bit players walked right into the novel and told me everything that I needed to know about them. But Dylan Caldwell, the photographer with whom Miriam was becoming romantically involved, eluded me.

It's his name, I finally decided. It's just too romance-novel-y. Somehow it just made him seem…well, less believable. Like he should be depicted bare-chested, all rippling muscles and Fabio hair on the book cover. Well, I could take care of that easily enough. I keep a name stash in my head…a sort of mental button jar…that I reach into and pull names out of when I need them.

In this case, the combo I fished out were the first and middle names of someone I'd seen briefly once I'd begun dating again, Daniel Joseph. The timing hadn't been right for us, and it had ended almost as soon as it had begun; but we were on friendly terms. Besides, his name had this great rhythm to it.

So Dylan Caldwell became Daniel Joseph, and the novel seemed to pretty much take off by itself. It was almost as if by changing my photographer friend's name, I'd tapped into this incredibly rich source of energy, and the whole book became suffused with it.

I shipped the new, improved *Souleiado* off to an interested publisher up in Maine. That was on Monday; on the following Friday, Lisl, a certified Chinese herbalist friend, handed me a card with the name Dan Clark and a Massachusetts phone number on it. I wasn't seeing anybody in particular just then, so I pocketed the card and figured I'd call when I got home.

Which I did, albeit somewhat half-heartedly. I was getting rather jaded on the whole subject of dating by this point and didn't expect much. Oh, good, an answering machine, I thought and rattled off a message. Later that evening, while I was putting the last remnants of the original *Souleiado* manuscript through the shredder, Dan returned the call. We talked for awhile and agreed to meet at a coffee place near my house. After I signed off, I happened to glance at the telephone's caller ID box and did one of my more spectacular double takes.

"CLARK, DANIEL J.," the smug little box flashed back at me.

Naw, it couldn't be, I assured myself and went over to the calendar to pen in our date. And despite the genuinely interesting phone conversation we'd just had, I was still more than half-convinced that this was just going to be another one of those "Kinda Sorta Awkward Meetings That Resulted in Nothing."

Which just goes to show how psychic I'm not sometimes. The coffee date I'd been half-dreading turned out to be two of the most pleasant hours I'd spent in a man's company in a very long time. Dan was a good talker and a good listener. He was intelligent, perceptive, and had a genuine warmth about him. He also had the most incredible eyes that were the luminous blue-gray of labradorite, moonstone's dark cousin. They talked even when he didn't. When he walked me to my car, we shook hands, and he said, "Call me if you'd like to talk again."

The eyes were what did me in. Something in them called to me, stayed with me all the next day or so until I finally gave in and called him. He came over with a videotape he'd rented; and when he said good-bye this time, he pulled me to him and gave me a kiss that melted me down to my bones and then some.

The next night when he called, I couldn't wait any longer and casually mentioned what the caller ID box had told me. "What's the 'J' for?" I asked.

"Joseph," he replied.

I had to tell him then, of course, and we had a good laugh over it. Actually, we've had a lot of good laughs over it and a whole slew of other things. For, you see, in a short time, we've become part of each other's picture. It's kind of hard to argue when the universe sends you such an explicit answer. The first model apparently wasn't the right one.

By T. J. Banks

T.J. Banks is the author of *Souleiado*, a time-travel novel. She has written fiction, poetry, book reviews and essays for numerous publications, including *Poets & Writers, Cat Fancy, Chocolate for a Woman's Heart*, and *Chicken Soup for the Single's Soul*, to name just a few. T.J. lives with her daughter, Marissa, their cats and two rabbits in Simsbury, Connecticut.

The Seat in the Window

Fate is an unexpected external intrusion that brings out the strength or the weakness in me. I decide if I am too weak in disaster or to re-assemble my life to divine contributions.

—Garnet Hunt White.

On the day I started my eighth month of pregnancy—a very difficult pregnancy that necessitated staying in bed most of the time—I was examined by my obstetrician, who gave me such a good report that my mother and I spent the afternoon picking out a layette. Tired from the shopping expedition, I lay down for a nap at my mother's house. When I woke up, I felt terrible pains in my abdomen, and as I stepped out of bed, saw that I was bleeding. My mother immediately called a taxi (that was before the days of 911) and took me to the hospital.

The baby, born by C-section, was a girl. I was told that she was perfect, but weighed only three pounds ("the size of a chicken," an insensitive neighbor remarked when she heard about the baby). I also was told that because she weighed so little, her chances of survival were only fifty-fifty. I couldn't see the baby yet because she was in an incubator, and I was too weak from my surgery and loss of blood to be wheeled to the nursery. I could only imagine what she looked like. But my husband had seen her, and he said she was beautiful.

During my second day in the hospital, my obstetrician told me the baby was "holding her own." But that night, I awakened from a deep sleep and heard a nurse say something that sounded like "The Uslander baby." That was all I heard, but something in the tone of her voice made me suspect that what I had been dreading so much had happened.

The following morning, nurses flitted back and forth in my room. They all asked how I was feeling, but not one of them said a word to me about my baby. And I was afraid to ask. The phone, that had been ringing continuously the day before, was ominously silent. There was no sign of my doctor.

At eleven o'clock, my cousin's husband, Bob, an intern at the hospital, came into my room and pulled up a chair beside my bed. He took my hand and said,

127

"I'm so sorry. She was a real fighter, but she was just too little to make it. Her tiny lungs gave out."

I didn't say a word, but from what Bob saw in my eyes, he realized that I hadn't been told. "Wasn't Dr. Reynolds in to see you?" he asked, an astonished look on his face.

I shook my head, no.

Bob took me in his arms and held me. My husband walked in crying. I couldn't cry. I just listened numbly as Bob and my husband angrily discussed the fact that my doctor had neglected to tell me that the baby had stopped breathing sometime around 2:00 a.m.

Nothing seemed real to me that day. Friends and relatives who had heard the news started calling to console me, and I spoke to them easily and rationally. I was still in shock. Thanks to a sleeping pill, I even slept through the night.

But on the following day, the grief began to grip me like a shroud. Though in a private room, I was still on the maternity floor. Through the open door, I kept seeing nurses bringing babies to their mothers to be fed. When the closet door opened, I saw the brown maternity suit I had worn to the hospital. I couldn't bear to look at it! As the day wore on, I felt worse and worse. I kept visualizing the room my husband had painted pale yellow for the baby. I kept seeing the white baby furniture, and the tiny little clothes my mother and I had picked out only a few days before.

During dinnertime, I was alone in my room. My husband had gone down to the cafeteria for a sandwich, and an orderly had left my dinner tray, which I hadn't touched. It was dark outside, and it seemed even darker inside. I started feeling very tense, agitated, as though all my nerves were standing on end. The idea of going home and seeing that empty bedroom; spending days alone in the house (having given up my teaching job to be a full-time mother), and perhaps worst of all, the thought of becoming pregnant again, and possibly going through this terrible nightmare *again*, filled me with absolute panic! I kept staring at the partially open window, and I broke out in a cold, sickening sweat. The open window was beckoning me.

Suddenly, the door opened. A good looking young man called me by name and asked if he could come in. I didn't recognize him at first. Then I realized who he was, a rabbi by the name of Richard Hirsch, who was a good friend of my father-in-law's. I assumed that he had been sent on an official mission, to talk to me about the death of my baby. But then he explained that his wife was in a room down the hall. She had given birth to a boy the day before. Richard had heard my name mentioned by someone visiting another patient, and he had inquired about me at the nurses' station.

Richard walked into my room and sat down on the window seat. "Are you cold?" he asked.

I nodded, and he reached up and closed the window. He stayed for about twenty minutes, telling me how sorry he was to hear about my baby. He said that his wife had lost two babies before finally giving birth to a beautiful, healthy baby boy.

He told me how thankful my husband and family must be that I was all right, because, apparently, my life had been in danger, too. And he assured me that time *would* ease the pain, and that like he and his wife, my husband and I would have a baby—perhaps many babies.

When Richard left, I suddenly felt much calmer. And I finally cried—not so much for myself and my husband, or for my parents or my husband's parents, but for the tiny baby who had fought to stay alive, but "just couldn't make it." Something in Richard's eyes, and voice—in the soft, gentle touch of his hands on mine when he said goodbye—finally allowed me to cry.

That was many years ago. I eventually gave birth to two wonderful sons, and now have three beautiful grandchildren. And yet, if not for that timely visit from the young rabbi, those sons and their children might not be here today.

Rabbi Richard Hirsch now lives in Israel. A friend recently told me that he was in town. "Do you remember him?" she asked me.

"Oh, yes," I said. "I remember him well." What I didn't tell her was that I will never forget how he sat down on the window seat in my hospital room and then closed the window. What I didn't tell her is that I have never gotten over the feeling that the young rabbi's appearance in my room *that night* was a case of more than someone just happening to be in the right place at the right time. I believe that Rabbi Hirsch was sent to be with me that night.

By Arlene Uslander

Blessed

Summer mornings are beautiful in Toronto. That morning was no different. I had brewed myself a cup of Earl Grey and was sitting in the kitchen with the community newspaper spread out on the table. Outside, the sun was just climbing the skies, and inside my home, it was pleasantly cool. I was enjoying watching the leaves of the oak trees in my garden rustle in the slight breeze.

In the newspaper, I noticed a small item announcing the arrival of Swami Shivananda from India. He was holding services in our temple, and many devotees were expected to attend. The paragraph read, "Swami Shivananda will be personally blessing forty statues of the God Ganesha. These idols will be available at the temple for devotees. The proceeds from this initiative will go to the New Beginnings Orphanage in Calcutta, India."

I had been collecting Ganesha idols for a long time. Looking over my collection, I felt a certain pride. I had Ganesha sitting, sleeping, standing and reclining; the elephant-headed God with his rotund belly and kind eyes was gracing my home with his presence in so many ways. Now I wanted one that was actually blessed by a holy person. I felt it would add a certain sanctity to my collection to have one blessed by the Swami.

With this objective in mind, I visited the temple in the evening after the function was over. Upon inquiring, I found it was not possible to buy one of the blessed idols. "Sorry, Ma'am, all of them were sold out within a few hours," one of the volunteers, a young man in a grey suit, informed me.

I felt a keen sense of disappointment as I sipped a soothing lemonade in a little juice bar outside the temple. Then I told myself that if one of those idols was meant for me, it would certainly come to live in my home.

The months passed, and I all but forgot about the special idol. Fall set in, the season heralding the beginning of the five-day worship of the Goddess Durga. I went to the temple and bowed low before the Goddess, who was resplendent in red silk and gold. I met many friends and spent time celebrating the festival. A deep sense of belonging to my community, of my roots, took hold of me during those five days. Listening to the devotional songs, inhaling the swirl of incense, and participating in the social activities kept me happily occupied.

Outside the temple, as in previous years, there were some stalls selling traditional items like incense sticks, saris and photographs of gods. One of my weaknesses is a love for knick-knacks. I greatly enjoy rummaging among them. I thought I might even pick up something for my collection. But since there was a fairly large crowd, I waited until the rush was over.

The owner, a middle-aged lady in a green sari, smiled, welcoming me into her stall. She had traveled all the way from India with her goods to be there that day. She was saying to the only other customer, "This is my first visit to Toronto. I like your temple very much!"

I marveled at the carvings of marble elephants, the wooden jewelry boxes, and the painted storks with sharp beaks. Once the other person had left, the store owner beckoned to me, "Would you like something special?"

I was quite taken aback. I nodded, and the woman disappeared under the counter. She brought out a tiny metal idol of Ganesha and held it out to me. "This idol was blessed by Swami Shivananda when he was in the temple this summer. It was given to me. It is for you."

She refused to let me pay for it, and I took my special Ganesha home, astounded by what Fate had dealt me.

By Moushumi Chakrabarty

Moushumi Chakrabarty is a writer, poet, mother and reader—just some of the multiple hats she wears in her life. She grew up in India and lived in Bahrain in the Middle East before making her home in Ontario, Canada, where she now lives. She has written since early grade school in diaries and journals, graduating to newspaper and magazine articles. Now, she writes mainly for online venues on topics as varied as parenting, the environment, writing and humour. She is the author of the e-book, *Positive Thoughts for Writers—Tips and Resources to Jumpstart Your Creativity and Make You Smile.*

The Wave

Fate…Forces that route your life on the proper course, from beginning to end. Life's ebb and flow and your place in it.

Skywriters. I used to watch them as a child.

High over my home in the San Fernando Valley, during the early 1960's, flying the old two-winged "biplanes" from an era now long gone, making magic against the vast blue, heavenly slate. Using their aircraft as though a pen; creating those enormous, puffed-white letters, of an alphabet I had yet to learn. Craftsmen in the sky, making larger than life those large, spacey messages, seemingly so trivial today. I watched them so long ago, floating across the apparent stillness of those crystal-blue California skies. "Scripture" they were, these banners driven slowly across the valley heights by winds aloft, delivering "Commandments" and "Messages," seemingly from God:

"DRINK COCA COLA"

"4TH OF JULY AT PACIFIC OCEAN PARK…"

"L.A. COUNTY FAIR, OCT. 1-31, POMONA FAIRGROUNDS"

In Sunny California, that's how one would note the season's change. The summers seemed to last forever…and so we'd drink our Coca Cola on the drive down to the beach, following Santa Monica Boulevard and the like-minded in their automobiles, who bottle-necked us at every stoplight for what seemed like a hundred miles!

We might stop at the Will Rogers Estate on the way to the beach, and look at the old house, or the grass polo fields where Wiley Post used to land his famous wooden airplane, the "Winnie May," long ago retired as an exhibit to a museum known as the "Smithsonian."

Then we'd head to Will Rogers State Beach.

"Boy! People sure liked Will Rogers! Hey, Ma! Who's Will Rogers?"

And then my brother Mike, my sister Chris, and I, we'd jump and dance in the surf; picnic with Mom on the beach; walk the shore at water's edge; look for sea shells in the foam; then try to recite stupid things like…"Sally sells sea shells

132

at the sea shore!" God only knows why, other than to laugh ourselves silly, while trying to out-do each other with our grand recitals!

Then we'd explore the barnacle-covered rocks beyond water's edge, looking for star fish, sea anemone, and octopi that would cling there in the waters of Santa Monica Bay…in a day when those waters were still clean.

Then Mom, her gentleman friend (since Dad had "up and split!"), and I would hang around in that warm, mellow evening breeze, beside that gentle bay that was friend to us all. A bay upon which stood two timeless wooden structures: the first, that massive, towering keeper of the rocket sled on wheels, the roller-coaster-laden Pacific Ocean Park pier; the second, the trendy, yet nostalgic antiquity at the end of Route 66, the Santa Monica Pier, where the merry-round forever twirled and the calliope music played; a tiny corner of my world where there was laughter under the stars.

That was back in a time when "Ike" was our President, when the summers were never ending, and life was good. These were among my first memories.

As was the summer I nearly drowned. The year was 1959, and I was three and a half years old. My brother, sister, and I were walking at the edge of the surf at Santa Monica Beach, looking for sea shells. As usual, we were letting the waves roll across our bare feet, as the tide caressed the shoreline. The three of us liked the feeling of motion we got when the surf returned to the sea…somewhat of a sinking feeling that seemed to drag you with it.

Mom had given us all the warnings, such as not swimming for twenty minutes after eating; otherwise, we'd get cramps and drown.

"Ma? What are 'gramps'?"

She, of course, warned us of the dreaded "Rip Tide." Personally, I thought he was a character from Grandma's favorite song, "Mack the Knife," or perhaps…a famous actor? (Come on, give me a break; remember, I was only three years old at the time!) In actuality, the Rip Tide was a strong, underwater current known as the "undertow" that exists when nearby storms of great strength create a hydraulic force that builds a sandbar near the shore. As the sandbar grows, the water in-between builds up until it overflows the barrier, then cuts a path back out to sea.

Working through physics, as though a "Venturi Tube," the pool of water passes through the channel, increasing velocity at the narrow point, before exiting the sandbar in a rush. A "ripping" is thus created—like a saw blade clearing through a piece of wood, becoming a device that can drag at first, then flow quickly, ultimately taking even the best swimmers out to sea very rapidly.

As it was, I didn't know how to swim. I hadn't wandered far from our mother when a wave came in, and I ran out to chase it back to sea. A big mistake, because the wave was followed by a second, larger wave, before the first had even retreated. That larger wave grabbed me like fingers curling on a hand, and proceeded to pull me right in.

The sensation of being tumbled in the sand, under the water, was as heavenly as it was frightening. I couldn't breathe; I was swallowing great amounts of water, and I could see my sister and brother trying to grab me from the sea, without being pulled in themselves. In fact, they were chasing me as the wave took me out towards the ocean. Neither could seem to catch up. My ears, immersed in water, could hear only the pouring, bubbling sound of the surf, and an occasional word or two my sister yelled to me through the brine.

I was running out of air and becoming weaker. I was scared, and yet the feeling was of being so airy and light. There was no feeling of suffocation; I would liken it to being in the womb, though I am hard-pressed to remember that far back! Just the same, I do think that was the closest I ever came to being in the hands of something angelic, though I did not see an angel.

Or did I?

I remember looking directly at my sister, and the effect was as though looking through a plate glass window with a waterfall rushing over it, and there she was—"big sister," desperately reaching out for me!

Then I heard her yell: "Grab my hand!"

I couldn't reach her; I was too weak. I made one last thrust and she caught my hand, clenched it, and pulled with all her might, dragging me from the wave. One hand trying to take me out to sea, the other trying to pull me back in to shore, and the smaller of the two hands won!

The reality of my situation was clear, as I gagged and spit up salt water; then began crying, my lungs once again filled with air! No doctor around, but I should have been slapped on the back!

My brother and my sister were laughing, while simultaneously scared to death! My sister said, "We almost lost you! You almost died!"

Forty years later, I still haven't learned how to swim. Go figure. I still love the water's edge, and I want to spend time on the open waters of the Pacific. Wherever I can find an ocean, a lake, a river, or even a stream, somehow, I can find peace there.

Only my Creator knows why…

By Mark S. Daniels

Mark S. "Bear" Daniels is a professional writer and photographer who manages Images of Light Internet Press Service at www.ilips.net. Daniels has been published by United Press International (UPI), Associated Press (AP), Reuters and others. While working as a photographer for United Press International, Daniels became only the second FAA-sanctioned photographer in the history of Air Racing to ride in an Unlimited Class racer during an actual air race competition. He is father to Christine Carol Daniels and Ida Renee Daniels, and the proud grandfather of Cody Allen Newton.

The Sisters

A white BMW rounded the curve in the night darkness, its headlights catching the silhouette of two standard poodles, running into the road. The driver was not going that fast, but a screech pierced the air as he hit the brakes; then a sickening thump sounded as the car pulled to a stop, too late.

As soon as my husband, Dick, let the poodles out of the van at the large, grassy field used as a dog park, they sprinted off in a direction they had never gone before. Thinking they must have been frightened by something they had heard, he started after them, but the black dogs blended into the dark of the rainy Thanksgiving evening. As Dick ran, he called their names, "Chien! BonBon!" but his voice was muffled by the heavy humidity. The dogs suddenly circled back into an area lit by a pair of street lamps, then darted into the road, quickly cutting back onto the grass, then heading into the road again, their long legs propelling them into the path of disaster.

Dogs are allowed to run free at the Coronado Cays park, and although it is unfenced, Dick had thought the poodles were safe unleashed because they were familiar with the area, and were usually very well-behaved. The Cays was their favorite place to play when we were staying at our condominium in Coronado, California. Dick would leave the side door of the van open, and the dogs would run back and jump in when they were ready to go. We were in Coronado now for the long Thanksgiving weekend, our last visit for the year. We had finished a turkey dinner with our neighbors half an hour earlier, and it wasn't that late, but dark descends early in the wintertime in Southern California.

Dick thought at first that both dogs had been hit by the car, but as he ran toward them, he saw only Chien, the male, lying on the ground. The driver and passengers were climbing out of the BMW. One of the passengers, an older woman, had started to cry. BonBon, the female, was prancing in circles in the road. Dick grabbed her by the collar and pulled her into the van. He then rushed to Chien who was badly hurt, and in shock.

As Dick gingerly lifted the 52-pound dog into the van with the help of a pass-erby who had been walking his own dog, Chien, crazed with pain, sank his teeth into Dick's hand, resulting in an injury that took weeks to heal. Chien had never bitten anyone before. Dick drove to the nearest animal hospital. BonBon, fright-ened and shaking, crouched in the front wheel-well of the van while Chien died in the back.

Dick, BonBon, and I each grieved in our own way over Chien's sudden death. Dick twice broke down and cried. I kept remembering Thanksgiving morning when Chien pawed at me, begging for attention while I worked at the computer, and how I had shooed him away. Now, I wished I had kissed him and told him how much I loved him.

BonBon was traumatized—she lay on her dog bed, starring straight ahead, for hours at a time. Chien was already a member of our family when three-month old BonBon had come to live with us six years before, and they had formed an instant bond, never thereafter being more than a few feet apart. They were extremely loving dogs—both toward each other and toward us.

Late Saturday night, we drove from Coronado to our home in suburban Phoe-nix. As we pulled into the driveway, BonBon became very excited. When we let her into the house, she ran from room to room, searching for Chien, sniffing and smelling his scent. When she did not find him, she took to her bed with one of her stuffed toys, or "babies," and rarely left the bed, day or night, except when she needed to go outside.

For years, BonBon and Chien had relished an early morning routine in our back yard of barking back and forth with the dogs next door. Fortunately, no other neighbors were close enough to be disturbed. Our property has a block wall around it, but if the poodles crouched down, they could peer at their pals through an opening under the wall where a wash runs between the two lots.

Now, when BonBon went out in the morning, she stood by silently while the dogs on the other side barked; she didn't even get down to look under the wall anymore. She ignored her favorite treat—Trader Joe's peanut butter dog cookies. And, when we got home from work (in the past, a joyous occasion with the poo-dles jumping up on us, barking and licking us), she stayed on her bed. It was very sad to see our previously happy-go-lucky BonBon, the dog that we always joked had a spring inside her, in this terrible state of depression.

Within a few days of Chien's death, Dick and I knew we had to get another companion for BonBon. For various reasons, we didn't want to start over with a puppy, so we decided to get another dog about BonBon's age. Chien normally had been such a well-behaved dog that we called him "The Little Gentleman." But, he had one bad trait—he disliked little dogs. He barked ferociously and pulled at his leash when a small dog walked by. We preferred to avoid what we considered to be "macho" behavior, so we agreed to look for a female, and we definitely wanted another black standard poodle.

We started our search for a six-year-old, female black standard poodle by con-tacting animal shelters and poodle rescue leagues over the Internet. We did not find *any* standard poodles that needed a home, let alone a poodle of our specifica-tions, although we contacted places as far away as LaJolla, California. Apparently, it is very unusual for a standard poodle to end up at an animal shelter or rescue league, and the breeders we talked to had only puppies.

A whisper of Fate stirred in my mind at some point during our search, reminding me that the breeder in El Paso, Texas, who sold us Chien and Bon-Bon, had said when we left the kennel with BonBon, "If anything ever happens, and you can't keep your dogs, call me, and I'll take them."

I reminded Dick of this and said, "Maybe she told other people that, too, and someone has brought back a poodle we could have." He didn't pay much atten-tion at first, but when we found no standard poodles closer to home, he finally looked up the breeder's name and called to see if she had any ideas about where we might find the dog we were looking for.

Brigitte Copeland had very sad news to impart. Her only daughter, a partner in her business, had died, and she was in the process of closing down Copeland Kennels, after 26 years, to go home to Germany to take care of her aging parents. She remembered both Chien and BonBon well. Chien was the runt of his lit-ter—too small to show—but she had planned to use him for obedience trials until we bought him when he was nine months old. Six months later, when Chien's mother was pregnant, we ordered a female puppy (BonBon) from the upcoming litter. Now, Brigitte had several standard poodles for which she needed homes before she left for Germany, including three females, Maggie, Lucy, and Angel, who were between the ages of six and eight.

Brigitte asked about BonBon's personality and said she would think about which dog might be best for us.

When Brigitte called back two days later, she suggested that BonBon might get along well with Maggie, a retired show dog. Maggie was a six-year old, female black standard poodle, *exactly* the dog we had been searching for! In fact, Fate had made sure there could not have been a more perfect companion for our dear, sweet BonBon. The dog named Maggie was BonBon's littermate. *Her sister!*

We flew to El Paso on December 18, 2002, to pick up Maggie, almost six years to the day we had made the same trip to pick up BonBon. Maggie is an American Kennel Club "finished champion," whose formal name is Champion Falkirk Hocus Pocus. She has had one litter of six puppies, two of whom are finished champions. She comes from a litter of six, four of whom are finished champions. While BonBon was living the life of a common pet, hanging out in our back yard with Chien, her sister Maggie had strutted around the show ring to the applause of the crowds. While BonBon, spayed at an early age, mothered stuffed toys, Maggie had nursed real pups.

When we put a collar around Maggie's neck to attach the leash to lead her from the kennel to our rental car, Brigitte told us it was the first time in Maggie's life she had worn a regular dog collar; that a show dog doesn't wear a collar because it will wear down the fur around its neck. Brigitte demonstrated how, when she wanted Maggie to do something, instead of pulling on her collar, she led her by the ears.

Dick drove the rental car from El Paso to Phoenix, with me sitting in the back, tightly hugging Maggie. We arrived home in the early evening and took Maggie and BonBon into our backyard to introduce them. They sniffed each other and got acquainted while on leashes; then were let loose. They were standoffish, but everything seemed to be going fine, until BonBon did a fast run around the yard and "body slammed" Maggie.

The body slam was a signal that BonBon was ready to play—it was something Chien used to do to BonBon when he wanted BonBon to chase him. Maggie, who obviously had never been body slammed before, turned up her nose at this somewhat crude behavior, and started to walk delicately back toward the house, walking straight into the swimming pool.

Maggie had not lived at a place with a swimming pool, so she didn't know that she couldn't walk on water. As soon as her front paws got wet, she realized what was happening, caught her balance and backed up, walked around the pool, and into the house, holding her nose high in the air.

Maggie's grooming put poor BonBon to shame. Maggie was coal black when we picked her up, even though Brigitte had described her to us ahead of time as having some grey in her hair, and BonBon was clearly greying. Maggie had a fairly simple poodle cut, not the fancy cut she would have enjoyed before she retired from the show ring, but she did sport a wonderful puffy pom-pom tail with a little ring shaved at the base of it, and cute little black toes stuck out from her shaved feet. BonBon had still a simpler cut and was overdue to be professionally groomed. I immediately got out a brush and started working on her.

At bedtime, BonBon lay down on her bed in our bedroom, where she sleeps next to a very large, floppy, stuffed bunny we bought when she was new at our house to give her a "mother" to cuddle up to at night. She stretched out her legs and strategically placed her front paws on Chien's bed, next to hers, to keep Maggie off, should Maggie decide to sleep there. But Maggie was not interested in sleeping on a dog bed. She was uneasy her first night away from the only home she had ever known, and she spent the night on the floor next to Dick's side of the bed. We wondered if she had ever slept anywhere but in a cage.

We took the poodles on leashes for a walk in the neighborhood the next morning. Maggie held her head high and glided along as though she were in a show ring; BonBon, harking back to her German ancestors, ran alongside the road with her nose to the ground, sniffing for game. Quite a contrast! We had to leave the dogs alone during the day while we went to work, but they were ignoring each other, so we were sure they would be okay while we were gone.

Dick came home from work early that day and took the dogs to the grocery store in what we call "the dog van," purchased specifically for the poodles. Chien and BonBon loved sleeping on the back seat, looking out the side windows, or lying on the floor between the captain chairs in front and being petted as we traveled along. Maggie apparently had never ridden in a vehicle except in a cage, so she was a little confused about what to do. She chose to lie on the floor—and traveled along, facing backwards.

Over the next few weeks, BonBon's depression disappeared, and Maggie's assimilation into the family became complete. Maggie was just as loving as Chien and BonBon had always been. The sisters became close friends, licking each other's faces in unison, running together to the wall in the backyard to bark at the dogs next door, and playfully taking turns sleeping on each other's beds. BonBon gave up body slams, perhaps because she was learning more dignified behavior from her more refined sister. For our part, we bought some professional "Black Star" color enhancing shampoo to take to our dog groomer, after which both dogs pranced around in coal-black coats.

Chien's death was the result of bad Fate, or being in the wrong place at the wrong time. If Dick had not taken the poodles to the Cays that night or had kept them on their leashes, Chien would not have died as he did. If Dick had arrived with the dogs at the park five minutes later, and the dogs missed hearing whatever it was that caused them to take flight, or if the BMW had not happened along just when it did, things might have been different. Chien might be with us today.

We also had good Fate, however, in that we found Maggie because we called Brigitte when we did. If we had called even a few days later, Maggie might have been sold to someone else, and a few weeks later, Brigitte would already have left for Germany, and the phone would have been disconnected. The two sisters, together at birth, separated and never expected to be together again, were reunited six years later in middle age to live out their lives together—due to Fate.

By Brenda Warneka

Wrong Trains, Wrong Stations

The bow is bent, the arrow flies, the winged shaft of fate.

—Ira Frederick Alderidge

At two o'clock in the afternoon that day, I stepped onto the train that would take me home to visit my parents in Singleton, England. I had been waiting for months to get a weekend off work and was more than a little happy to finally be heading home for a few days.

I sat down and opened my book, ready to waste away the two-hour train trip. Luckily, the book was engaging, and time passed quickly. An hour into the trip, I was interrupted by the guard checking people's tickets. I rifled through my things and finally found it in my back pocket, handing it to the impatient guard.

"Singleton," he said, "You're going to Singleton?"

"Yes," I said. "I am."

"But you're on the Dungog train."

"What?"

"You're not on the Singleton train."

"You've got to be kidding."

"I'm sorry, I'm not."

"But I have to be in Singleton today."

"Well," he said, "I don't think you can do much about it now. You can't switch; you can only go back to Newcastle, but you already will have missed the last train for Singleton."

"So what do I do?"

"Stay on the train; take it to Dungog. Then go back where you started."

"No—this can't be happening."

"The next train to Singleton is at five o'clock in the morning and then another at 9:00 if that helps."

"No, not really," I mumbled.

The guard apologized, asked if I was all right, and then wandered off to check on other passengers' tickets. I sat there silently cursing myself. How stupid could I have been? Granted, I was new to the area and hadn't taken the train before, but still, it was not that hard to get on the right train. After another half hour berating myself, I accepted that nothing could be done about it and settled in for the trip to Dungog, and back.

A few hours later, I was standing back at the platform I had started at, still angry with myself. I stumbled the two blocks home to my flat, dumped my bags inside the door, and lay down on the floor.

"Hey, you're here!" said my flatmate, bounding into the room like she had all the energy in the world.

"I'm here."

"Weren't you heading home?"

"I was," I said. "You wouldn't believe it—I got on the wrong train."

"You're kidding."

"No, I've been sitting on the train for four hours, just to go to Dungog and back."

"You poor thing. But don't worry. I have just the thing—come to Maitland with me!"

"Maitland?"

"Yeah, Michael told me Friday nights they have great Karaoke at this bar there."

"I don't think I'm in the mood for it."

"Come on; I'll buy the drinks. I have cash. I worked your shift today—remember?"

"I don't know if I want to go."

"Come on, what else are you going to do?"

That's how I ended up at a bar in Maitland on a Saturday night, sitting alone, sipping a vodka, while my flatmate entertained the crowd with her singing. That's when a cute young soldier named Tony walked up and offered to buy me a drink.

While chatting, I asked him what he was doing in Maitland. He explained that he was on exercise in Singleton and had meant to catch the train into the city for a night out. He and his mates weren't from the area and had assumed Maitland was a section of the city and got off there, only to find out it was a different town, and one with not much of a night life. That's how he ended up talking to me in a Maitland bar.

A drink later, and Tony asked me to dance. My friend winked at me and sang a slow one for the next number. I closed my eyes during that slow dance, and right then, I knew. There was a natural rhythm between Tony and me, and somehow, it felt right. The dancing, the conversation, everything. Somewhere in that dance, he kissed me, and then it was certain. This was the man I had been waiting to meet my whole life. I just knew it, and a few months later, he admitted that he had known it, too. My flatmate admitted what I already knew—she hadn't taken me to that bar because the Karaoke was good; she had taken me to that bar because nobody else sang Karaoke there, and she knew she could be the star for the whole night.

For two years, Tony and I got to know each other while living in different cities and alternating weekend train trips to see each other. Then one day, I waved good-bye to him at the station and stepped onto the train to head home. I took a seat and opened my book to read. That's when I heard a voice saying, "May I check your ticket please?" Except instead of a ticket inspector, it was Tony. And instead of holding out his hand for the ticket, he was holding a diamond ring. "How would you like to take a ride with me," he said, "for the rest of your life?" Of course, I said yes.

And that is how our paths crossed. Thanks to me getting on the wrong train, and thanks to him getting off at the wrong station. There were a lot of wrongs in the way we met. But in the end, everything turned out as right as it could ever be.

By Mishel Hawas

Mishel Hawas is a writer and poet based in Australia. She lives in a small country town with her husband and spends her days writing articles, stories, essays and poems. Her work has been published in various anthologies, magazines and e-zines.

Nothing Beats a Failure
but a Try

I have wanted to be a writer since I was ten years old. Even at a young age, as I observed the world around me, I felt a deep awareness and understanding of the human condition. In 1992, I self-published my first book, *You Can Be*. I was working at a full commercial printing company and was given a great discount. One day a customer came in and said she was looking for a person to work at her publishing company. She talked to a co-worker who was a graphic designer, and they made an appointment to meet for lunch.

When the customer left, I said, "I'm going to apply for the job. I have always wanted to be in the publishing industry." The co-worker, who had become a friend, burst into laughter and told me that I could never work at a publishing company, reminding me that I didn't have a degree, nor was I a graphic designer. Even though I had already published, I lacked self-confidence, and I took her words to heart and didn't pursue the position.

My friend went to lunch with the owner of the company and returned with nothing but complaints about how the meeting went. She made several ludicrous assumptions about the woman based on that one-hour meeting. I listened to her but refused to accept only her account of the meeting. I found the publisher to be charming and intelligent.

I was the only black woman on the office staff, and was told the day I was hired that there had never been a black person in the front office before. The business had been in existence 42 years at that point. An awful racial incident then happened at the printing company. The owner had recently hired the first Hispanic in the company, and one of the pressmen was extremely prejudiced against Hispanics. Things escalated, and I found that I could no longer work for the company and maintain my self-respect. So, one day in August of 1993, I quit. I walked off the job and never looked back. I decided that I wanted to further my education and enroll in college. I gave myself nine months to rejuvenate and make plans for my future.

The time off was marvelous. I spent a lot of time with my son and learned to love having leisure time. I also began a lifestyle change that culminated in a weight loss of 78 pounds. In January of 1994, I began classes and felt strongly that I was on the right path. I wanted to write and work with writers. My nine months was up in April of 1994. Almost nine months to the date, I picked up the *Evanston Review* newspaper to search for a part-time job.

My eyes immediately fell upon an ad seeking a part-time person to work at Evanston Publishing, the company owned by the woman I remembered from the print shop I had worked for. I took a chance and sent her a personal note, and she responded by calling me in for an interview. The moment I walked in and saw all those books, I knew I was home. She hired me on the spot.

My background in printing turned out to be better than a college degree. Even though I still had no talent in graphic arts, I excelled at collections, customer service, and the day-to-day operations of running the business. It wasn't long before I was hired full-time. I had been working for the company for three years when the owner announced that she and her husband were relocating to Louisville, Kentucky. At first I was devastated. Here I was, working at my dream job, and it was being taken away from me.

I then overheard the owner talking to someone and telling her that she was planning to keep the business. I spoke up quickly and told her that if she was going to keep the business, I would relocate with her. She accepted, and I moved my family to Louisville. The move turned out to be the best thing I have ever done in my life. Although I had tried to break into the world of writing for magazines and newspapers in Chicago, I was unsuccessful. It was just the opposite in Louisville. Within a year, I had my own column. I also began acting and directing plays, and have given several speeches. I received the Distinguished Citizen Award and the Key to the City from Mayor David Armstrong.

I laugh every time I think about how my so-called friend tried to discourage me from pursuing my dreams. Some people believe in luck; not me. I know that there is something greater working for my good, and the good of us all. We have to be open, ready, and willing to recognize the opportunities for success that greet us each and every day of our lives. Nothing beats a failure, but a try. Believing and being patient paid off for me.

By Wanda Johnson-Hall

Wanda Johnson-Hall is an award-winning free-lance writer and performing artist. She lives in Louisville, Kentucky, with her husband and three children. Wanda is the author of two books of poetry, *You Can Be* and *I Am Not A Poet,* as well as her autobiography, *Telling the Truth and Shaming the Devil.* She writes a monthly column for a syndicated magazine, *Today's Woman,* and for several local magazines and newspapers. In 2003, Wanda was selected as the first place winner in the "Scenes and Dreams" contest, sponsored by the City of Louisville Metro Parks Division for her essay, "The Power of Memory."

A Whisper in July

It was about ten years ago in July. The Willamette Valley in Western Oregon was caught in the grip of a balmy, sultry summer. I woke up perspiring, and went to bed wearing saturated, sticky clothing. The only reprieve was sitting under a fan, on high speed, or standing under the pulsating stream of tepid water in the shower. As a result, I was taking more showers than usual, which also meant more laundry.

Being relatively new to the Portland area, I was living with my best friend, Elena, while trying to get settled. We routinely did mundane chores like laundry, cleaning the cottage, and shopping on the weekend.

Since it was Sunday, we were heading off once more to do the laundry together. We'd just gotten everything sorted by color, and packed the baskets and detergent into my car, when a telephone call came. It was about Elena's second daughter, Emma, who was 14 and lived with her father and two older siblings. Emma had started a fire and was being taken to a youth facility for evaluation.

Elena immediately left for the youth facility, leaving me with the mountain of laundry to do on my own. I went to a Laundromat we had used dozens of times. One of the reasons we frequented this particular Laundromat was because it was rarely crowded. Not only could we get our laundry done faster, but also we avoided the assortment of unsavory characters, complete with unruly kids, that frequently seemed to go with the territory.

On this Sunday afternoon, there was no one at the Laundromat but me. I began the tedious task of feeding the hungry washers with clothes, quarters and soap. Then I plopped myself down on one of the plastic orange chairs that ran the length of the shop, hugging both walls. There were a few outdated magazines strewn on the counter that was over the middle row of washers. I grabbed a *Good Housekeeping*. Maybe I could learn something useful. So what if it was a couple of years old?

The washers growled to life. In the distance, I could hear lawn movers. The hum of the machines and the heat of the day made me sleepy. I wanted to go home and take a nap under the steady blast of my rotating fan.

In the midst of the washing, I saw a white van pull up outside. But it didn't park; instead, it backed into a space on the corner that provided the occupants a clear view inside the Laundromat, and parked there, motor running. At first I didn't think anything of it, but then I realized the two men in the front seat were watching me. There was no way of telling if there were others in the back of the van.

Since it was still daylight and only mid-afternoon, I normally wouldn't have been that concerned, but an uneasy feeling, like I was being stalked, came over me. The longer they stared, the more nervous I became.

There was no back door to the place. The only exit was through the front, which would undoubtedly mean a confrontation. I began to look around for something I could use to defend myself against an assault. There was nothing but two small wastebaskets and my laundry baskets, neither of which would offer me much defense. Even the chairs were clamped together with a solid bar.

I was acutely aware of the men's presence, but I tried to pretend I was casually reading the magazine, waiting for my clothes to dry. One of them got out and went around to the back of the van. Fear swept over me like a warm breath.

I wished, over and over, that I hadn't chosen such an isolated place. If only Elena had come with me. My heart sank; there wasn't even a phone inside. The nearest pay phone was outside, perched like a solitary soldier on the corner of the parking lot. It wasn't going to do me any good that far away.

I kept telling myself not to panic; to remember every detail in case I had to recite them later to the police. All I could tell at this point was that the person on the passenger side was a white man with dark hair. Sunglasses hid his eyes. I could not see the driver's face. If they weren't up to mischief, why hadn't they brought in their laundry? Why were they watching me? There were no good answers.

As time slipped away, late afternoon shadows inched closer to the Laundromat. The sun was low behind the clouds, as if it didn't want to see what might be coming. Tension was twisting a knot tighter and tighter in my stomach as I retrieved the last of my clothes from the dryers. Soon there would be no excuse to stay inside. I would have to confront these men, this situation, whatever it was. I prayed it wouldn't be lethal.

Just then, Elena's metallic-gray Sundance pulled up outside. I felt as though a moment of reckoning had taken place, like miners must feel when rescued from the jaws of a granite death in a chasm of blackness. She came into the Laundromat, seemingly oblivious of the situation, as simultaneously, the van started to move, and then its back doors flapping recklessly, sped away. Slowly, I released my breath. I was safe now.

Elena looked at me, her hazel eyes holding mine. "What's wrong?" she asked. "Did you see that van?" I asked. She nodded.

As I recited my story to her, she listened in a way that let me know she understood how close this brush with danger had been.

"I just knew in my gut that they were up to no good, and there wasn't going to be any way of avoiding them, until you came," I finished, thankful for the happy ending.

"I would still be there with Emma, but another patient didn't show, and they took her right away," Elena said. "I almost went back to the cottage, but something told me not to. I had this feeling that you were calling for me."

"Well, I've never been so happy to see you in my life," I said half-laughing, half-crying. We quickly took the laundry out and loaded it into my car. Instinctively, I looked for the van, but it was gone, and I was not to see it again.

I will never really know what those men intended to do, but it had to have been bad. There was something, whether cosmic or divine, that stepped in and whispered to my friend that I needed her help.

By Katherine Marsh

Katherine Marsh is a Dutch-American free-lance writer. Her work has been published in many magazines, journals and anthologies, including, *Painting Daises Yellow; Lynx Eye; The Palo Alto Review,* and *American Profile Magazine.* She is also the author of the anthology, *Voices From the White Noise* and the sci-fi thriller, *The Male Model.*

Some Kind of Miracle

Everything comes gradually at its appointed hour.

—Ovid.

My mother had been in a deep sleep for three days, taking in no food at all, and a minimum of forced liquid. A "Do Not Resuscitate" sign hung over her bed. Every time I looked at the sign, I shuddered. The finality of the words chilled me, even though the heat in her bedroom was way too high.

She was 88 years old and had reached the end of a long illness. She was still in her own apartment, but I had arranged for round-the-clock nursing care for her; I did not leave her side during those three days.

On the fourth morning, a Sunday, I called my husband and asked him to pick me up and drive me home (some forty minutes from my mother's apartment) so that I could get clean clothes. I had been wearing the same pair of jeans and blouse for four days, having had no idea when I arrived that the end was so near.

As we drove home that Sunday, my husband and I decided that before we went back to my mother's apartment, we would stop at the funeral home to make arrangements. The doctor had said that she would not last more than a few days at most, and the previous evening, the visiting nurse agreed with his prognosis. We felt it would be better to make the funeral arrangements while we were still relatively calm, rather than after the emotional trauma of death had set in.

I also wanted to stop at the grocery store so there would be some food in the refrigerator for the nurses and myself.

Once at my house, I quickly showered and dressed, then threw a few clothes into a shopping bag. We got back into the car. Suddenly, I told my husband that I had changed my mind about stopping off at the funeral home. And I did not want to take time to buy groceries, either. Something inside me told me that we had to get back to my mother in a hurry—before it was too late.

I rang the bell in the lobby and the daytime nurse, Callie, buzzed me in. After the elevator ride up to the 22nd floor, I saw Callie at the end of the hall, a look of

151

amazement on her face. "It's some kind of miracle!" she exclaimed. "Your mother's eyes are open!"

Hurrying into my mother's bedroom, I was shocked to see that her eyes *were* open. She was propped up in the rented hospital bed, staring straight ahead. At first, I thought she was dead, and my heart started racing. But then she shifted her gaze and looked straight at me. She had a puzzled, questioning look on her face, as if to ask, "Where am I?" Or, perhaps, "Where am I going?" Then a grimace passed over her face—a grimace that I have replayed in my mind over and over again. Was it a grimace of physical pain? Of fear? Of sadness? I think by then, she felt no more pain, so it must have been a combination of fear and sadness—deep sadness at leaving, and fear of the unknown. She needed the comfort of being in my arms when she began her journey.

I held her frail body gently, and spoke to her softly, telling her how much I loved her. And then I could feel, and see, that she was gone.

I asked Callie how long my mother's eyes had been open before I arrived.

"Only a few minutes," she said. "When I heard you ring the bell downstairs, I said to your mother, 'There's your daughter. Now you just hold on there. Don't you die before she gets here.' And she *did* hold on. She waited for you."

Thinking about the fact that something told me not to stop for anything on the way back to my mother's apartment, but to hurry as fast as I could; thinking about the fact that my mother opened her eyes when I rang the bell, and kept them open until I got there, so that I was able to say goodbye to her, I suspect that Callie was right. It *was* some kind of miracle. It was the Hand of Fate.

By Arlene Uslander

The Curve

When I awoke in the morning, I anticipated that something ominous was about to happen, with dark clouds everywhere; but, when I pulled back the curtains to look outside, the clouds disappeared into a bright sunny day. The morning went along smoothly, the clouds forgotten.

Later that afternoon—summer time, Florida, 1998—I got into my car, shutting the door and turning on the engine simultaneously. As a rule, I am not a particularly cautious driver, but I did check to see that the path was clear before I backed out. Then I sped away. That is a good word for it, sped; my foot was heavy on the pedal.

It was not a good idea to drive fast in this Central Florida countryside. People came here to live because it was still a comfortable drive to the city. A lot of these people had children. I knew I should be careful, but in the back of my mind, there were no death warnings that day. All thoughts of the morning's dark clouds had vanished.

I took the hills at top speed, feeling the rise in my stomach. When I turned, heading west into town, a car appeared in front of me. "Where did it come from?" I wondered aloud. I always talk to myself, believing it is a sign of intelligence, not craziness. What *was* crazy was a car appearing out of nowhere.

The car in front of me was barely moving. The old man or woman driving (I could not tell which from the back of the head) was short, barely reaching the steering wheel, and had gray hair. The old model car was from the fifties. I tried to pass. Darn! The car swerved out, and I was not able to get by. "I'll show you," I muttered, as I tried again to get around the car.

Cut off again! For some reason, the car in front of me would not allow me to pass.

I turned my attention back to the road. We were close to the large curve, the one with the flashing warning light. I slowed down. When I got around the curve, I would pass the old car with its antiquated driver.

I suddenly saw a car barreling around the curve in the wrong lane! I could hear the squealing of the brakes. It managed to swerve into its proper lane, just missing the old car in front of me. I felt my foot on the brake. In front of me, the old

153

car slowed and disappeared around the curve. I took a deep breath. In my mind, I could see what would have happened if I had managed to pass the old person in front of me. I would have arrived at the curve at the same time as the oncoming car came around it, in my lane. I would have been hit head-on. The old car in front of me had held me back, and saved my life. I would enjoy traveling behind it now. Maybe I would get a chance to wave or flash a smile at the driver.

I came around the curve. The car *was gone*. How was that possible? There was nowhere to go. After the curve, the road was straight—no side streets. I could see a mile or two up the road, all clear. The car had simply vanished. I thought back to the clouds of the morning. The car had disappeared just like the clouds!

By Ann Lucas Peters

Ann Lucas Peters teaches Spanish at a private elementary school, and is a free-lance writer. She is the author of *Inspirational Thoughts for Living, an A-Z Guide for Life,* and the web site "Ann's Attic." Ann has lived in and traveled to many countries. She now makes her home in Florida with her two daughters, two dogs and six cats. She believes in angels that interact on our behalf.

Was It Luck or Something Else?

Lisa and Sal Pipitone of New York City were visiting Las Vegas over the weekend as guests at a ceremony honoring her brother, a 9-11 victim of the World Trade Center.

As the Pipitones walked past a row of red, white and blue all-7 slot machines at Green Valley Ranch on Friday, Lisa, who was born on July 7, later told friends she felt strong vibes to play the slots.

Her brother, Don DiFranco, was among six New York TV transmitter engineers who died when the twin towers collapsed. The Pipitones were among 17 family members who were guests Saturday [August 24, 2002] at the Nevada Broadcasters Association Hall of Fame dinner, which included a tribute to the engineers.

Lisa, in retelling her story, said she knew what machine she wanted to try, but the next seat over was taken, so she decided to return when she and her husband could sit side by side.

They came back later, found her machine, and the two started playing. Almost simultaneously, they hit jackpots.

They took their winnings to the cashier cage and were stunned when a cashier told them they had just won a total of $911.

"Lisa believes absolutely that it was a sign from her brother," said Bob Fisher, president and CEO of the Nevada Broadcasters Association.

By Norm Clarke

Dispatched

The following is a true story of fate. Names have been changed to protect those involved. A friend of mine, a police officer, shared his story with me. Read on to find out how two men find themselves in the wrong place, at the wrong time.

November, 1992

After a one-year assignment in the Detective Bureau, Officer Tom Howard, a veteran of many years with the police department, found himself back on the streets, working as a training officer. A rookie officer rode with him for the first part of his shift. Howard worked Shift Two, from noon to 10:00 p.m., and the rookie's training officer wasn't on duty, so rather than have him sit around at the front counter doing nothing, Howard took the rookie with him for the first part of his scheduled duty.

At around 5:00 p.m., he dropped the rookie off at the station and went back out on patrol as a solo unit.

It had been dark about an hour when he was dispatched to a silent burglary alarm covering the back door of a health food store.

Sounds from the police radio broke the silence in the patrol car, "David 2,459 silent at 1098 North Main Street, Griswell's Health Foods. Covers the back door."

"David 2, Copy." Howard wrote down the address in his steno pad. *Not much has changed,* he thought. He remembered going out on calls to that same store when he was on patrol before. The neighborhood knuckleheads had a habit of kicking in the back door to break in. Heading in that direction, he began thinking of the layout of the store, and a plan of action for when he got there. He knew better than to approach the call as routine. It didn't matter how many false alarms the dispatch unit received, the next one could be the real thing.

"David 2, 10-97." He let dispatch know he'd arrived on the scene.

"David 2, 10-4. Advise on backup."

Pulling his police car unit into the dirt lot adjacent to the south side of the store, he eased the nose of the car close to the corrugated fence which separated the two lots, and got out. He walked to the front of the car and stepped onto the front bumper so he could look over the six-foot-plus fence and get a view of the back door of the store. It stood wide open.

"I've got an open rear door. Send a backing unit," he told dispatch.

"David 2, Copy."

Walking east to an area where it was easier to climb over the fence, he hurtled over into the back lot behind the health food store. On the other side, he found himself behind a couple of rows of ice cream trucks that blocked his view of the store. Moving forward a few steps, he peered between two trucks and spotted a man coming out the open door. A bright light over the rear entrance shone down on him. The man, who appeared to be in his late forties, wore a pair of black slacks and a white dress shirt open at the neck, with his sleeves rolled up. His right hand gripped the butt of a gun he held in front of him. Howard pointed his flashlight in the man's direction and yelled, "Stop! Police! Put the gun down!"

The man looked at Howard and hesitated, but said nothing. Then he walked toward an older black Lincoln sedan that was parked near an old dilapidated building at the back of the property. He never took his eyes off Howard. *Very unusual behavior. Why doesn't he answer?* Howard thought. By now, the man had moved within fifteen to twenty feet of him. Howard yelled out again, "Stop! Police! Put the gun down!"

Nothing!

A silhouette of a second man appeared from inside the rear entrance of the store. He had not yet stepped out into the light over the doorway, and Howard couldn't make out any details of his appearance. *Great, now there are two of them. How many more are inside?* he wondered.

The silhouetted man quickly went back into the building. The white-shirted one with the gun momentarily turned his back to Howard. He then turned around and took a small step toward him. Gripping the gun in both hands, he raised it up, pointed, and shot one round. Howard was hit in the chest and the impact through his Kevlar vest knocked him back against one of the trucks. He shot two rounds at the man as he fell, but the bullets missed his target.

Righting himself, Howard found a spot behind another truck to take cover. He positioned himself so he could contain the shooter and watch him more easily. Then he let dispatch know about the shots fired. He yelled again, "Police! Put the gun down!"

Howard felt a burning sensation in his upper chest. Something sharp poked him. Reaching his hand up, he undid his uniform shirt and looked at his Kevlar vest. A dime-sized jagged hole showed through the corner of the choke plate (a thin metal plate that slides into the vest and covers the middle of the chest). His T-shirt and vest had blood on them. The bulletproof vest had stopped the bullet, but the sharp edges of the damaged plate cut into his skin.

Exhaustion overtook him. *When will this nightmare end? When will he stop shooting at me?* By now, the man was standing up on the porch of the old dilapidated building at the back of the property. He shot two more rounds at Howard. Returning fire, the policeman realized that he had somehow hit his target. He watched as the man took a few hesitant steps back from the doorway and collapsed in a heap.

Sirens whined in the distance. Howard heard officers calling out that they had arrived at the scene. "In the back of the store," he advised over the radio. Still, none of the back-ups showed. *Why is it taking so long for them to get here?* He knew he was in bad shape from the blunt trauma of the bullet to his vest.

"We're at the entrance of the building," he heard the response, and seconds later, two officers came barreling through a gate into the back yard.

Finally, the two officers checked on Howard and after he gave them a fast update, he stumbled out the open gate, telling dispatch, "I'm going to retreat."

The paramedics were waiting in the dirt lot near his black and white. They put him on a stretcher and cut his shirt off to get at his wound. One of the officers on the scene, Officer Jones, stayed while they worked on Howard.

Later, Jones got quiet, and Howard asked, "What's going on?"

"He's dead," Jones said.

Howard thought, *The man tried to kill me. He had every opportunity to leave, but instead, he started shooting at me.*

"He was the store owner's brother."

"What? He never said a word. All he did was look at me." Howard paused. "Why didn't he say anything? Why did he shoot at me?"

Epilogue

The local newspaper told the whole story the next day.

At 7:00 p.m., the previous night, Officer Tom Howard was dispatched and responded to a silent burglary alarm at a health food store, but went to the wrong location. As a result, he ended up at an ice cream business. He was engaged in a horrific shootout and was hit in the chest. His Kevlar vest stopped the bullet and saved his life.

The report went on to say that the store owner's brother was not as lucky. He came out of the rear of the store, a nine-millimeter handgun in his hand. Despite Officer Howard's continual demands to put the gun down, the man proceeded to open fire on the officer. Howard returned fire, and the store owner's brother died at the scene.

According to the newspaper article, no one knew why the man opened fire on Officer Howard, but because the ice cream business owner and his brother were from the Middle East, speculation was that they didn't understand what Howard had said and thought they were being robbed. The irony of the tragedy was that the dispatched call was for Griswell's Health Foods' new location; the business had moved from the old location only two months before. And, the alarm from the health food store's new location that evening was false.

Both men would have been better off being somewhere else that night. Even though dispatch put out the burglary call for the new address, and Howard wrote the address down correctly, he responded to the old address from force of habit. The manager and his brother, according to what police found out later, were on their way to put the day's earnings and receipts into a safe in the dilapidated building at the back of the property.

Much later, Howard discovered that the man who shot at him had been a police lieutenant in his native country. What were the odds of two police officers, from different countries, having a shoot-out? What were the chances that a bullet fired from Howard's gun would ricochet off the vinyl-covered hard top of the black Lincoln and into the center of the man's back at the exact moment he turned to enter the old building?

What would have happened if Howard had had the rookie with him? He assumes they would have ended up at the correct address. Or would the rookie have been involved in the tragedy, too?

Howard spent some time in the hospital. The black and blue bruising that covered his chest was a telltale sign of the amount of impact the bulletproof vest had taken.

Four days after the shooting, the dead man's family filed a wrongful death suit in federal court. During the original case, affirmed in the appeal that followed, the jury found that Howard had not been negligent, even though he went to the wrong location.

Ten Years Later

Today, Officer Tom Howard still feels regret over the whole ugly incident. So many questions remain unanswered. Why did force of habit send him to the wrong address? Why did the man shoot at him? Howard has spent many sleepless nights, wondering about the shooting, and the only answer he can come up with is that the gunman didn't believe he was a police officer. "He must have thought I'd come to steal his money," he reflects. "Maybe he couldn't see me clearly." Howard will never know the answers to his questions. And he will never have closure.

He says, "It's not like on television and in the movies. I was involved in a gun battle, was shot and lived. I killed a man. It wasn't glamorous."

By Susan Lynn Kingsbury

Susan Lynn Kingsbury is a freelance writer whose articles have appeared in publications such as *Cruising World* magazine, *Writing Etc.*, and *The NAWW Writer's Guide*. She also writes two monthly columns, book reviews and news stories for a local boating newsletter, the *Arrowhead Log*. When she's not working on short stories, essays and columns, she concentrates on her book projects which include a police procedural manual, focusing on corruption within city government and a nonfiction book, *From a Woman's Point of View, My Husband's Love of Sailing*. You can find her at hometown.aol.com/writingsbysilk.

"My New Family"

At nineteen, Mac, a tall, slim, dark and handsome young man with piercing black eyes, was the "wild one" in a family of eight children. His parents were never able to successfully discipline him in the mores and traditions of the early years of the 20th century. He was my dad's brother.

It was the period just prior to the First World War, and the social transition that followed. Mac wanted to taste as many of life's fruits as possible. He never deprived himself of the opportunity to follow whatever path tempted him—no restrictions. Just prior to his twentieth birthday, he met and married Helen Harris, after a brief courtship. In time, Helen gave birth to a beautiful baby boy, strikingly in his father's image.

However, the bonds of marriage proved too binding for Mac, and Helen found it difficult to cope with Mac's need to spread his wings. After he strained at the bit for a while, they separated and divorced. Helen proposed that he need not support them on the condition that he give her complete custody of their baby. Freedom to roam beckoned, and Mac, however reluctantly, finally agreed to the arrangement she set forth.

In 1917, the glamour and excitement of WW I captured the imagination of young Americans. Mac enlisted and shipped off to France. He nostalgically recalled the army songs, camaraderie and the French girls for the remainder of his life. Those were carefree and happy years for him, despite having been wounded in the war. During his last days, a WW I song still brought a smile to his eyes.

While Mac was away, Helen moved and left no forwarding address, even changing the spelling of their last name (Joseph, to Josef) so Mac or his family would not find them. His letters never reached them, and he was unable to locate his child. Bert was lost to Mac and our family. He was two years old when Mac left. Helen and Bert changed residences frequently while Bert was growing up; he never understood the motivation behind the many moves. His mother told him that his father had been killed in France. She was a bookkeeper, and later worked as a beautician.

In time, Bert completed his education and grew to manhood in a lonely environment. Helen never remarried, and she even kept him apart from his maternal aunt and cousins. She did not encourage close relationships.

Mac moved to California after returning from France, and married again. Sylvia, his lovely new wife, gave birth to two daughters, Judy and Carol—two sisters Bert never knew existed. Bert married Pearl Gorin while living in New York. They also had two daughters, giving Bert his first real family. He was overjoyed.

Bert's aunt finally convinced Helen to tell Bert about his father. It was then he learned the shocking truth, that his father had not been killed in France, and that his original name was Joseph. Helen said she had no knowledge of Mac's whereabouts or whether he was still alive. The truth created a barrier between Bert and his mother; he even changed the spelling of his name back to Joseph. But, he enjoyed his wife and children, and his job as Foreman of the Mechanical Unit of the U.S. Post Office kept him busy until his retirement.

After their daughters married, Bert and Pearl decided to move to Florida. He contacted his friend, Michael Goffredo, in Orlando, Florida, to let him know he was coming down to complete arrangements for buying a condominium in Fort Lauderdale. The Goffredos invited him to spend some time with them before going on to Ft. Lauderdale.

A few days after Bert called Michael, Mac's sister Bess, of Orlando, 80 years young and doing her daily jogging, passed Goffredo's apartment.

"Hey, Bess, come on in for a cup of coffee," Michael called to her. Fate at work.

She went up, and wept as she told them that her brother Mac had recently passed away in California. During the conversation, fate seemed to put words into Mike's mouth.

"Bess, what does the initial 'J' in your name stand for?" To this day, he doesn't know what made him ask that at that moment.

"Why, that's my maiden name, Joseph. Why do you ask?"

"Frankly, I don't know why, but that is a coincidence. I have a friend whose last name is Joseph. Bert and his wife are moving to Florida." The name "Bert" alerted her.

"How old is your friend?"

"Oh, I guess he's about 62; he just retired."

She couldn't contain her excitement. Was it possible? She asked for Bert's phone number. A phone call confirmed Aunt Bess's wildest dream: Bert was indeed Mac's long-lost son. After 60 years, he was returned to our family. He brought with him his birth certificate and his parents' marriage certificate. Bert and Pearl were surrounded by a delighted, loving family who had all gathered to meet them, almost in disbelief.

When my husband and I, who live in California, arrived in Florida, and approached the condominium where they lived, I had no problem picking out Bert from the other people standing in front of the building. Looking at him, there was no doubt that he was Mac's son. The Joseph genes were there.

During our initial conversation, he said: "I was stunned, shocked, and surprised from the moment I learned that my dad had been alive all those years, and then I found I had a large wonderful family with two sisters I never knew existed." He shook his head as though to make sure he was awake. "I'm very proud and humble that such an amazing thing could happen to me," he said with great emotion. His wife told us he feared he would wake up and find it was all a dream. She said that a whole new world had opened up for him.

The Bertram Josephs have three grandchildren, the fulfillment of Bert's dream of having a family of his own. Now he has added to his family cousins by the dozens, as well as his two lovely sisters.

Uncle Mac's photos adorn every area of their home—photos sent to them by all of the family, and the album of our relatives is entitled "MY NEW FAMILY."

By Florence J. Paul

Florence J. Paul has been published in 53 magazines, internationally, and is the author of four books: *Peg, a Dream Betrayed* and its sequel, *Leah's Dream; I See the World*, and *He Never Pulled the Trigger*. Florence is the recipient of several awards from California Press Women. She is a community activist, fully responsible for the completion of a one-mile linear park and walkway. The mother of two sons, her grandchildren are her greatest joy.

On the Wings of Love

I married young, while still in high school. A faithful wife to a husband whom I found to be a cruel man, it was a miserable and frightening existence. When I graduated from high school in 1997, I attended community college for a year before the stresses of my daily life ripped away my ability to concentrate. That single year of college was the only time during the entire relationship when I felt free to express myself. It seemed to me that my husband was bent on destroying me by abusive and manipulative behavior.

College was where I met Robert—a shaggy-looking boy with a Beatles haircut. We conversed only one time, but we both wrote poetry, and felt drawn to exchange our notebooks of verse. Robert was a truly gifted writer. I returned his poetry notebook through a mutual friend at school. After that, I didn't see him for two years.

When we met again, it was at my home, during the summer of 1999. I had finally left my husband and invited friends over to celebrate. Robert tagged along with them on that wondrous Fourth of July. I fell in love instantly, but denied it for the entire week following the encounter.

Finally, I relented, knowing from my caller ID that he had been trying to reach me. I telephoned and asked him to come over to my place. We danced and talked until 4:00 a.m. Saturday morning, but before I allowed myself to get in any deeper emotionally, I made him leave. I pushed him out my front door, telling him to go home and get some sleep, then call me when he woke up. He hugged me over and over, but I told him we were going too fast.

At ten o'clock that morning, I called his home, unable to wait any longer to talk to him.

His mother answered.

"Is Robert there?" I asked, cheerfully.

With a sob, she replied, "We've been trying to reach you."

I froze. "About what?"

"Robert's dead!" she wailed.

Bolts of lightning shot through me. I reeled. How could this be? Weren't we falling in love just six hours ago?

Robert's mother and I must have discussed some things after that. I'm sure I asked what happened, and I know I rambled on about how Robert had not done anything wrong that night, and how sorry I was. It was then that Robert's best friend took the phone, and explained that Robert had never made it home from my house. He had been in a car accident. They had been trying to reach me since they found out, but my phone had been busy; I had been playing an online game on the Internet that morning. I was dizzy with emotion.

Six days, I thought. I had met him two years before, and it all came down to six days during which I spoke to him once on the phone and saw him twice. I attended his funeral. I was introduced to all the people I didn't know as his girl-friend. He didn't look right, so still and quiet in his casket. A young man, so full of life and talent, and love for everything.

Robert had told me (and this was confirmed by his best friend after he died) that he had never in his short 21 years drank or smoked or touched drugs of any kind. He died driving over 90 miles an hour on a slick, dark road. I know how it happened. He was as happy, excited, and elated as I was. He died from love.

By Nicole Allen

Nicole Allen was born and raised in a small town in central Mississippi. In her mid-twenties, she enjoys reading, writing poetry, which she is compiling for a future publication, and listening to music. She also enjoys an active family life.

Norman

Synchronicity opens the door; fate is what happens if you walk through it.

—*Laurie Shelton*

It didn't mean much to me then—he was just one of hundreds of classmates I'd had in my life. But now, twenty years later, I still wonder if I will ever be able to thank him for what he did for me.

In the early eighties, computer programming become the hottest, most promising career for which young graduates could aspire. I wasn't a young graduate anymore, after working for the university for a number of years, and shifting from academia to the computer industry would be a major leap for me. However, like the new graduates, I was looking for a more promising future.

I enrolled in a COBOL class, the revolutionary programming language at that time. The computer school was a small one, with ten to twenty students per class. Most of my classmates were new graduates with business, accounting, or arts degrees. We were all eager to find a high-paying job in information technology.

After a few days of lectures, the class was divided into study groups for hands-on programming assignments. We were told to volunteer for the groups, five members to each one. Some of my classmates were already friends from college, or from other computer classes, and readily formed their teams. I didn't really know anyone, so I waited until a group asked me to join them.

I noticed that one of my classmates was also sitting alone; also waiting for a group to invite him to participate. He was very quiet, rarely raising his hand to recite. He always sat at the back of the room, and didn't seem to have any friends. He had a slight handicap—his left arm was deformed. It hung from his shoulder like an underdeveloped limb. His self-consciousness made the rest of us feel uneasy talking with him. I was sure no one disliked him, but at the same time, no one seemed to be comfortable around him.

Someone finally invited me to join their study group, and since it still needed a fifth member, I asked the loner to join us. He said his name was Norman.

Our group was the first to submit the hands-on exercise to the teacher. We had been quick to divide the work among ourselves, and Norman's exceptional

166

logic skills contributed largely to the team's flawless output. He and I became friends.

Toward the end of the COBOL course, Norman called me aside, and said he had found a recruitment ad for programmers. A leading computer service company was hiring immediately. Norman wanted both of us to send in our applications. I hesitated because there was one more course I wanted to take before looking for a job: Fortran, another computer language.

Norman wouldn't take no for an answer. He went on to say that a friend had told him that this company was good and paid well. "We can't let this opportunity pass!" After dodging him for days, I finally agreed—only because he insisted we go there together.

The company's Human Resources Manager met with us, and gave us application forms to fill out. Since Norman and I were ready with our bio-data and college transcripts, he told us to come back in seven days for our first screening-IQ tests. If we passed the cut-off score, we would be given a programming aptitude test, then a case study for panel presentation. It was going to be a tough screening process, but according to the HR manager, "That's because we hire only the best."

Norman and I left the building, excited over the prospect of working for one of the more well-known computer service companies. I reminded him that I wasn't sure about going to work so soon, with very little practice in programming. He wouldn't listen. He kept saying it was a good break, and that we should pursue it all the way.

Our COBOL course was finished, and since Norman wasn't enrolled in Fortran, I wouldn't see him again until our IQ test. As we parted, he casually said, "See yah!"

I was a little early for the test, partly because I wanted to get accustomed to the environment, and partly because I wanted to wish Norman good luck. The HR manager appeared, and ushered about thirty applicants into the examination room. I was the last to enter because Norman hadn't arrived.

We were informed that there would be a three-hour exam and that it would take fifteen minutes to check all the papers; then the aptitude test would follow. I kept wondering what had happened to Norman. I went outside during the fifteen-minute break to see if he had just been late, and was there, waiting for me. He wasn't.

At the end of the break, the HR manager came back to read off the names of those who were qualified to take the aptitude exam. I was one of three; the others were excused. A few days later, I was called for the case study and panel presentation. A week after that, I found myself being introduced to the Vice President and the Division Manager to whom I was to report. My new career had begun at last—and Norman was nowhere to be found.

I visited the computer school to look for him, but they hadn't seen him for a long time. I called the only phone number he had given me, but all I was told was, "There's no Norman here." I anxiously waited for him to call me, or to suddenly appear at my office to tell me why he hadn't taken the exam. As months passed, I sensed, with feelings of regret, that I wouldn't hear from him again.

I went on to work for that computer service company for fifteen years. Each year was better than the last. I mastered numerous skills, and learned many valuable lessons. It was a most fulfilling career.

As I signed my retirement letter, I remembered Norman—the person who led me to this path. I may never get the chance to thank him, but this I know is true: there have been many "guiding angels" in my life, and Norman was one of them.

By Ruby Bayan

Ruby Bayan is a free-lance writer published in print and online. She writes the "Inspirational/Motivation" column at www.Suite101.com and maintains an award-winning homepage, www.OurSimpleJoys.com, where she archives links to her published work and offers writing, editing, and site design services.

Fawn's Choice

It had been a little over a year since our dog Rex had passed away at the ripe old age of seventeen. We were fortunate to have had him with us that long. We weren't sure we wanted to get another dog, become attached, and then go through the painful, but inevitable, process of losing a beloved pet again. However, we finally decided that our household was not complete; it was time to get another dog. Although we had seen several dogs that we had warmed up to right away at an animal shelter, my husband, Dennis, was not interested. He said we should get a Great Dane who had "been mistreated and really needed a good home."

"Honey, what are the chances of our getting a dog with such specific requirements—a Great Dane who has been mistreated?" I asked. "Pretty slim, don't you think?"

"Well, we have to try," he said. "That really is the kind of dog I think we should get."

We didn't talk about it anymore.

On our way home from a Las Vegas vacation to Yuma, Arizona, where we live part of the year, we stayed overnight at a motel in Prescott. The next morning, Dennis went to the motel restaurant to have coffee; I remained in the room. I turned on television, something that I rarely do that early in the day. The program was "Pets on Parade," sponsored by the Phoenix Humane Society, showing animals that were available for adoption.

Near the end of the show, a Humane Society representative said, "We have one more dog who will be at our special adoption tomorrow, but we could not bring her today. She has just been spayed and is recovering from the surgery. This dog will need someone who can handle a very large dog and also be able to administer medication and meet the needs of her special diet." This really piqued my curiosity. (I later found out that the "special diet" consisted of feeding the dog small meals three times a day, and in addition to her dog food, she would need to be fed home-cooked items, such as eggs and vegetables. It was a lot more complicated than just pouring food from a bag or a can into a bowl.)

At that moment, a picture of the dog appeared on the television screen. I could hardly believe my eyes. It was a Great Dane! Her name was Fawn. Was this a coincidence or what? Could this be the dog Dennis had been talking about?

The picture of Fawn was pathetic. She was so skinny and sad looking. The announcer then said that Fawn was two years old and was recovering from starvation and beatings.

I started to cry, and said out loud, "Fawn, we will come and get you tomorrow."

Just as the program went off the air, Dennis walked into the room. He took one look at me and asked, "What's wrong? Why are you crying?"

I said, "Honey, remember the Great Dane you were talking about? Well, I know where she is."

"What are you talking about?" he asked.

I told him about the program I had seen on television. Dennis was overwhelmed. I asked him, "Did you have a dream about a dog like that? What made you say that you wanted a Great Dane who had been mistreated?"

Dennis replied, "No, I didn't have a dream. I just thought about the fact that there are dogs who have been mistreated and need good homes. I figured we would look for one who really needs us."

"But why did you say it should be a Great Dane?" I asked.

"I don't know; maybe because Rex was part Great Dane, and he was such a wonderful dog."

We called the Phoenix Humane Society to find out more about Fawn. The only thing we were told was that this was a special case, and that if we were interested in adopting Fawn, we would have to go through an investigation, which would include giving our social security numbers, and references. It sounded like a criminal background check. Also, the Humane Society would check with our veterinarian regarding our ability to care for a large animal with health problems. Not unlike what people go through when they want to adopt a baby! We gave them the necessary information.

We were told that there had been many telephone calls about Fawn after the television broadcast, and that if there were several interested parties present at the adoption, a drawing would take place. The winner would then be checked out to see if he or she qualified to adopt Fawn.

Sunday morning, we drove to the Humane Society. The adoption program was to begin at one o'clock. The hour and a half drive from Prescott to Phoenix seemed endless, as the minutes slowly ticked away.

Fawn was the last animal to be put up for adoption. There were about twenty people interested in her. Many of them left when they saw how pathetic the dog looked. A Humane Society officer paraded Fawn around the group. She stopped by Dennis. The officer tried to pull her away, but she sat down and would not move. It was as if she were saying, "This is who I pick!"

Through a process of elimination by the Humane Society officers, the final count was down to six. Dennis was in this group. The officers handed out numbered tickets, putting the matching stubs in a box. The officer then had a person from the audience draw the winning ticket stub.

The officer read the winning number. Dennis yelled, "That's my number!" Then he stooped down and hugged Fawn, who was still at his side. She gave him a great big sloppy kiss.

The officer took Dennis's ticket to make sure the numbers matched. They did. He then shook Dennis's hand and said, "Congratulations, it looks like this is a perfect match. Fawn certainly likes you, and I can see that the feeling is mutual. And by the way, we already did our investigation. Take Fawn home."

Was this really a coincidence? Why did Dennis mention a Great Dane as being the breed of dog we would take in? Why did I turn on television that particular morning, and why was it tuned to "Pets on Parade"? Was this fate after all?

By Colleen Kay Behrendt

Colleen Kay Behrendt lives with her husband and their beloved canine companion. She has two adult daughters and one stepdaughter who have blessed her with seven grandchildren. During the summer, Colleen and her husband reside in Northeastern Minnesota, and during the winter, in Southwestern Arizona. Colleen considers herself fortunate to be able to live in what she considers the best of both climates, as well as two of the prettiest regions of the United States. She is a member of the Desert Writer's Club in Wellton, Arizona. Her other interests are traveling, fishing, reading, animals, learning all she can about computer skills, knitting and crocheting.

The Man on the Flying Trapeze

Fate is when you let your heart steer your course instead of your head…and it makes all the right choices—whether you know it or not.

—Rusty Fischer

I became a professional dancer while still a teenager in high school; during the summer, I danced in the grandstand review at state fairs. The grandstand review was like a vaudeville-type show with specialty acts; unlike today, where a rock and roll star or a country western singer is the entire show. Singers and dancers, like myself, performed in large, flashy production numbers. Dancing was my whole life back then.

After I graduated from high school in June, 1953, and worked state fairs again that summer, I returned home to Chicago. Several dancers had heard about an open call for auditions, and my roommate, Kae, and I went to the rehearsal hall and did our best. We were told that our names were put on a list, and we would be called as opportunities for dancers arose.

In the meantime, I had to make some money. Thanks to my typing and short-hand classes, I was able to quickly find work in downtown Chicago in a one-girl office for a small company. The work was pleasant, and the pay substantial for those days—$55 per week. Since I was still living at home, my paychecks went to pay for my ongoing dance classes. I lived for the day when my name would come up on the list, and I would be called to work as a dancer.

Then one evening in mid-October, I received a phone call asking if I was interested in working six weeks, from Thanksgiving to New Year's Day, at a nightclub in Ohio. I would receive room and board, plus a fairly decent salary. I was ecstatic! My dream had come true. I rushed around the house, giddy with excitement, as I announced my wonderful news. But my mother soon put a damper on my enthusiasm. "It's only for six weeks," she said. "After that, what?"

"Then I'll get another dancing job."

"But there's no guarantee. And if you can't get your old job back, you'll be out of work again."

"Maybe they can hire someone on a temporary basis until I get back. They like me, and I'm efficient."

"Be realistic. If they find a good replacement, they'll keep her. How are you going to pay for your dance classes?"

My mother was right. Downhearted, I phoned the choreographer back and told him I had to refuse his offer. He unkindly informed me that if I wasn't willing to take a job when it presented itself, he would take my name off the list. I begged him to give me one more chance, maybe a longer engagement, but he refused. I cried myself to sleep that night, certain that I had permanently destroyed any chance I had of ever dancing professionally again. Why, oh why, had I listened to my mother?

The next month was barely tolerable. All I could think about was the great opportunity I had passed up. I could have been in Ohio, dancing my heart out, sharing wonderful experiences with my fellow performers. I was totally miserable. I knew I had made the biggest mistake of my life.

Then one afternoon, Kae, my former roommate, called me at the office. "How would you like to join the circus?" she asked.

"Sure," I said. "I can be the Fat Lady."

"I'm serious," Kae said. "In their new season, the Shriner Circus is going to have a line of eight dancers do an opening number, introduce two of their acts, then do a big finale. I'm going to audition."

"I don't know," I hesitated. "Give me some more details."

"Seventy-five dollars a week, straight pay, not pro-rata, and we work 46 weeks. Just think! If we save our money, in one year we'll be able to go to New York and try to get into some Broadway shows."

That convinced me. Even my mother agreed it would be worth quitting my job for such an opportunity.

Kae and I auditioned, were hired, and rehearsed throughout the Christmas holidays. In mid-January, we found ourselves in Flint, Michigan, for the beginning of the new season. The day before we opened, we had one last rehearsal. The auditorium was bustling with various performers practicing their craft.

Some of the younger men eagerly watched as we dancers went through our paces, and we found out later that in circus tradition, this was "choosing day." Single men would check out the eligible prospects and "make their choice."

That evening in the hotel dining room, I saw a young man walk in and speak to a woman who I knew was part of the show, so I assumed he was a fellow performer. He was blond, and he wore a trench coat and a porkpie hat.

I nudged Kae. "See that man over there?" I said. "He looks like he might be from Sweden, or Norway, don't you think? I've never dated a foreign man before, and he's really handsome." Another dancer overheard our conversation and immediately left our group to return with "the foreign man." Much to my embarrassment and his amusement, she introduced us.

"Walter, this is Sylvia. Sylvia, this is Walter." I took one look at his even white teeth, his beautiful smile, and his large blue eyes, and I immediately fell in love. I used to ask my mother how I would know when I fell in love, and she would say, "You'll just know." Boy, was she right!

As it turned out, he was a member of The Ward-Bell Flyers, trapeze artists. We were inseparable from that day on, and he later told me he had chosen me on "choosing day," warning the other young men to stay away. A year later, I married "the man on the flying trapeze." We had a daughter, Suzi, and eventually retired from the circus, and he became a stagehand for one of the major television networks. We shared almost nineteen years together as a happy family until his untimely death at the young age of forty five.

Many times, throughout the years, I have wondered what my life would have been like if I had taken that job for six weeks in Ohio. I never would have met Walter, and without him, I wouldn't have my wonderful daughter.

And, by the way, Walter wasn't from Sweden or Norway. He was a Hoosier from Southern Indiana!

By Sylvia E. Hand

Sylvia Hand, raised in Chicago, became a professional dancer at age sixteen. At the age of 19, she married and joined the flying trapeze act. Retiring from show business at a young age, she actively volunteered at her daughter's school and for the Girl Scouts. She and her second husband have traveled extensively and are now retired and living in Arizona, though still traveling as often as they can. Sylvia is a free-lance writer, having been published in magazines, and has written two juvenile fantasy novels and a humorous adult novel.

Epilogue:
Earthshakes

It was January 17, 1994. Depending on what a person happened to be doing, or where they happened to be, the earth moved in two very distinct directions that day.

If you were my wife on that morning in 1994, and just happened to sit down to play a few quarters in a progressive slot machine in the back lobby of the Golden Nugget Casino in downtown Las Vegas, you would have been in for a very pleasant surprise.

But, let's change the venue for a moment. Suppose that instead of being in a casino in Las Vegas, you were driving on a freeway in Los Angeles at a certain time in the morning. If that were the case, you would be in for a very different surprise.

In Las Vegas, for my wife, the earth shook in a minor way when three of the same symbols lined up in the right position of a slot machine in the lobby of the Golden Nugget Casino, and she instantly won $12,000.

That same morning in Los Angeles, some other individual had a very different appointment with fate when maybe on the way to work, the earth shook in a very real way, and the freeway, heaving from a massive earthquake, parted in a wide gap. The overpass in front of that driver, which a few seconds before had to have been as firm as rock to handle all the traffic it did, suddenly disappeared, collapsing onto the highway below it. And that individual, driving his or her car, went catapulting into mid-air where the overpass had been.

Two people, on the same day, in two different places, had their lives change, either for better or worse, because the earth shook at a precise time.

You ask, "What's the point?"

Let me continue. The following year, 1995, my wife and I were at the same convention in Las Vegas that we had been at the year before when she hit the jackpot. On the morning of January 17, in the main casino at Bally's on the Strip, after eating a leisurely breakfast, my wife stopped to play a roll of quarters in a progressive slot machine. A few pulls later, four symbols lined up in the right sequence, and she won over $475,000. Weird, isn't it? Two mind-boggling wins in two successive years, *on the same day of the year*, defying unimaginable odds, to garner close to half-a-million dollars. But wait, that's only part of it.

On that same day in 1995, again the earth shook twice: a minor tremor in Las Vegas, where my wife won almost a half-a-million dollars, and another full-fledged quake in Kolbe, Japan, where many people either lost their lives, or had their lives changed forever. Now, after the glow of the past excitement has worn off, I often think back on both of those days with mixed emotions, recalling the rush of elation and disbelief at defying the Las Vegas odds twice. I think about the revelry, telling our friends, who were there with us at the same convention, about our good fortune. And my wife calling our kids back home, who after the first announcement of the winnings, wouldn't believe her. I recall the lavish celebrations afterwards on the Las Vegas Strip, recounting the events of a lifetime with any stranger who would listen. And after that—after the formal celebration—our personal celebration back at our hotel room, into the small hours of the morning. Then, the two of us, lying there satisfied and comfortable in our bed, falling asleep close to each other, surrounded by the luxury of our hotel room, never once thinking about all of the other lives that had been changed in so many different ways on those two unbelievable days.

Fate runs in streaks, both good and bad, sometimes confusing us in a hodge-podge of seemingly unrelated happenings, though always driving toward some destination reserved for all of us, its unsuspecting subjects. I truly believe that Fate knows no boundaries. It works indiscriminately, demonstrating its control over everyone.

By Jerry Bower

Jerry Bower is a farmer from Clinton County, Michigan, who considers himself a "modern day adventurer." He loves to fish, hunt and explore, seeking out places where he can't see utility poles, concrete or other humans. He is the author of many short stories and is presently working on his first novel. He also writes poetry. He says that he often finds the inspiration for stories in remote places. "It's like when I'm in the right place at the right time that a story just pops into my mind." His favorite quote is an old Indian saying, "If one sits still long enough, the trees will speak and the dead will come visit." He thinks he may be looking for that place where it is possible for him to stay put long enough.

0-595-30283-1